A PATHWAYS IN GEOGRAPHY
Resource Publication

National Council for
Geographic Education

TEACHING

POLITICAL

GEOGRAPHY

**Fiona M. Davidson,
Jonathan I. Leib,
Fred M. Shelley,
Gerald R. Webster,
Editors**

The PATHWAYS IN GEOGRAPHY series has been
created by the Special Publications Advisory
Board of the National Council for Geographic
Education to support the teaching and learning
of themes, concepts, and skills in geography at
all levels of instruction.

PATHWAYS

PATHWAYS IN GEOGRAPHY SERIES TITLE NO. 19

Teaching Political Geography
Fiona M. Davidson, Jonathan I. Leib, Fred M. Shelley, Gerald Webster, editors

For information about this title or about the series:
National Council for Geographic Education
16A Leonard Hall
Indiana University of Pennsylvania. Indiana, PA 15705

ISBN 1-884136-15-x
Printed in the United States of America

Contents

Illustrations

Contributors

Shira Birnbaum, Department of Educational Foundations and Policy Studies, Florida State University, Tallahassee *(Chapter 12)*

Brian W. Blouet, Department of Government and School of Education, College of William and Mary, Williamsburg, Virginia *(Chapter 2)*

Stanley D. Brunn, Department of Geography, University of Kentucky, Lexington *(Chapter 5)*

Fiona M. Davidson, Department of Geography, University of Arkansas, Fayetteville *(Chapters 1, 4, co-editor)*

Colin Flint, Department of Geography, Pennsylvania State University, University Park *(Chapter 3)*

Douglas Deane Jones, University of Houston, Clear Lake, Texas *(Chapter 9)*

Janet E. Kodras, Department of Geography, Florida State University, Tallahassee *(Chapter 6)*

Jonathan I. Leib, Department of Geography, Florida State University, Tallahassee *(Chapters 1, 8, co-editor)*

Christopher D. Merrett, Illinois Institute for Rural Affairs, Western Illinois University, Macomb *(Chapter 11)*

Scott R. Myers, Department of Geography, Florida State University, Tallahassee *(Chapter 15)*

Alice T. M. Rechlin Perkins, Committee for Research and Exploration, National Geographic Society, Washington, D.C. *(Chapter 13)*

Arlene M. Shelley, Department of Geography and Planning, Southwest Texas State University, San Marcos *(Chapter 14)*

Fred M. Shelley, Department of Geography and Planning, Southwest Texas State University, San Marcos *(Chapters 1, 10, co-editor)*

William D. Solecki, Department of Geography, Montclair State University, New Jersey *(Chapter 12)*

Gerald R. Webster, Department of Geography, University of Alabama, Tuscaloosa *(Chapters 1, 7, co-editor)*

CHAPTER 1
TEACHING POLITICAL GEOGRAPHY

Fiona M. Davidson, Jonathan I. Leib,
Fred M. Shelley, Gerald R. Webster

The essays in this volume originated at a day-long symposium on the teaching of political geography presented at the annual meeting of the National Council for Geographic Education (NCGE) in San Antonio, Texas in October, 1995. In three paper sessions and an informal round table discussion, political geography teachers and researchers from around the United States met with prominent specialists in geography education and addressed relationships between political-geographic research, teaching political geography, and the recently published National Geography Standards, as articulated in *Geography for Life* (1994). The essays and discussion presented in this book are complementary to the March-April 1997 issue of the *Journal of Geography*, edited by Christopher D. Merrett and, like this volume, are devoted specifically to the teaching of political geography.

The San Antonio discussion focused on the implementation of Standard 13, "How the forces of cooperation and conflict among people influence the division and control of earth's surface." As Merrett (1997) has pointed out, political geography has in recent years emerged as one of the most important, dynamic, and exciting fields within the discipline of geography. Although many undergraduate geography curricula include courses in political geography, even more importantly, concepts developed in political-geographic research have emerged as important components of course syllabi in other types of geography courses at the college and pre-college levels, including world regional geography, geographies of specific regions of the world, cultural geography, human geography, urban geography, and economic geography. The teaching activities and lesson plans described in this book are relevant not only to formal courses in political geography but to many other types of geography courses as well.

The utility of the ideas presented in this book is not limited to college-level teaching. The ideas developed in political geography research have also influenced curricula at the pre-college level. *Geography for Life* contains extensive analyses of how teachers can use all of the National Geography Standards in developing and implementing elementary, middle, and high school curricula. The discussion, analysis, and lesson plans included in this book should inform teaching political-geographic concepts at all levels of education. We encourage teachers to build upon this foundation and develop new and innovative approaches to instruction on these and related topics.

The Renaissance of Political Geography

Chapter 4 of *Geography for Life* is devoted to "the subject matter of geography." This material is organized into 18 standards, each of which articulates a particular sub-field of geographic inquiry. Standard 13, entitled "how the forces of cooperation and conflict among people influence the division and control of Earth's surface," is directly relevant to contemporary research by political geographers.

Standard 13 represents a helpful summary of the scope of contemporary research in political geography. In examining how teachers can apply Standard 13 to teaching political geography, it is useful to consider the intellectual development of the field over the course of the twentieth century. Early in the twentieth century, much of the intellectual impetus underlying political geography was associated with the development of geopolitics, or the interface between politics, geography, and foreign policy.

The development of geopolitical theory was especially important in Germany. During the 1930s, Adolf Hitler and other leaders of Nazi Germany used the ideas of the German *geopolitik* school as intellectual justification for Nazi territorial expansion and the extermination of European Jews. Although contemporary historians doubt that German geographers involved in the development of geopolitical theory deliberately intended to influence Nazi policy, the taint of association between geopolitics and the Nazis retarded the development of political geography for nearly thirty years after World War II ended.

During the 1950s and the 1960s, quantitative methodology revolutionized geographical inquiry. In part because political geography had been discredited during the Nazi area, political geographers were slow to apply quantitative methods to their research. The combination of association with a discredited ideology of the past and the lack of linkages between political geography and quantification led the well-known geographer Brian J. L. Berry (1969) to dismiss political geography as a "moribund backwater" within the developing scope of geographic inquiry.

In contrast, the 1970s, 1980s, and 1990s were a period of renaissance in political geography (Reynolds and Knight 1989; Merrett 1997). During these decades, political geography advanced from a backwater position to intellectual leadership within contemporary human geography. Several factors are associated with political geography's recent rise to intellectual prominence. During the early 1970s, a younger generation of scholars trained in quantitative techniques began to apply these methods to questions of traditional importance in political geography, including the geography of elections and representation (i.e., Archer and Taylor 1981). These early contributors to the renaissance themselves were not trained directly in political geography, but rather in quantitative urban and economic geography. As they turned their attention to political questions, they began to train new generations of scholars whose work focused explicitly on political geography. Political geography came to be linked with other facets of quantitative geographical thought.

At the same time, research in geography became concerned about problems such as civil and human rights, environmental degradation, and lack of economic development in the so-called Third World. In order to develop a geographical perspective that would inform understanding and solutions to such problems, political geographers began to investigate theories of uneven development, world-systems theory, and other perspectives linking analysis of specific events to global perspectives. As geographers began to investigate these theories in more detail, they began to recognize that such approaches were inherently political. Political geographers began to link these theories to various topics of historic interest in political geography. Reynolds and Knight (1989) summarized these developments and their influence on geography as a discipline.

Several developments have symbolized the renaissance of political geography, including the establishment of an important international journal, *Political Geography*, in 1982 and the establishment of large specialty groups emphasizing political geography by the Association of American Geographers, the Institute of British Geographers, the International Geographical Union, and other important professional organizations. Much of the important research undertaken by political geographers in recent years has been published in *Political Geography* and other major geographic and interdisciplinary journals. The major threads of intellectual inquiry underlying this large volume of important research are included and summarized in these journals and in important textbooks (i.e., Demko and Wood 1994; Taylor 1993; Glassner 1996; Shelley et al. 1996).

National Geography Standard 13

As previously indicated, the thrust of National Geography Standard 13 is "how the forces of cooperation and conflict among people influence the division and control of earth's surface" (*Geography for Life* 1994: 90). Standard 13 emphasizes the interface between forces of cooperay stating: "The geographically informed person has a general understanding of the nature and history of the forces of cooperation and conflict on earth and the spatial manifestation of these forces in political and other kinds of divisions of Earth's surface."

Geography for Life identifies political divisions as "regions of Earth's surface over which groups of people establish control for purposes of politics, administration, religion and economics" (1994: 90). Countries, states, counties, municipalities, and administrative regions qualify as divisions. In the contemporary world, the entire inhabited land surface of the world is divided according to the principle of state sovereignty; that is, the international community recognizes each portion of territory as under the formal control of a particular country. Wars and international disputes throughout history have occurred as a result of disagreements over sovereignty and because of the failure of the state sovereignty principle to link states with nations, or groups of people defined on the basis of common cultural, linguistic, ethnic, or religious characteristics. Political geographers have long recognized the interaction between global interdependence and local initiative. As *Geography for Life* (1994: 91) concludes, "Students must understand the genesis, structure, power, and pervasiveness of these divisions to appreciate their role in a world that is both globally interdependent and locally controlled."

Geography for Life goes on to consider how teachers can apply this standard at three different levels: from kindergarten to fourth grade (K-4), at the middle school level (grades 5-8) and at the high school level (grades 9-12). Fourth graders, for example, should understand how people divide Earth's surface, know different types of territorial divisions at different levels from local to global, and describe how cooperation and conflict affect places in the local community (130-131). They should be able to identify and describe different types of territorial units, describe characteristics of political units at different scales, explain how and why people compete for control of Earth's surface and analyze current events as examples of cooperation, conflict, or both.

By the end of middle school, according to the standards, students should be able to understand how cooperation and conflict contribute to political, economic, and social divisions of the earth's land surface and to understand territorial divisions (169). Students completing middle school should be able to identify different types of spatial divisions such as school districts, telephone area codes, and voting precincts, explain why people cooperate as well as engage in conflict over control of the surface of the earth, and describe and compare factors affecting the cohesiveness and integration of particular countries.

Finally, *Geography for Life* argues that high school graduates should understand "why and how cooperation and conflict are involved in shaping the distribution of social, political, and economic spaces on Earth at different scales" (210). They should also understand the influences of multiple spatial divisions on people's daily lives, and how self-interest and ideological conflict affect conflict over territory and resources. Accordingly, they should be able to analyze how cooperation and conflict influence the development and control of divisions on the earth's surface, understand how external forces (such as the changing world economy) affect internal characteristics of divisions.

How can the renaissance of political geography and the implications of Standard 13 be translated into the effective teaching of political geography? Julian Minghi first addressed this question more than thirty years ago. His long and distinguished career has spanned the entire renaissance of political geography from backwater to forefront and his research and teaching has played an important role in the renaissance of political geography.

During the 1960s, as Minghi (1966) pointed out, political geography was seldom taught, especially at the pre-college level. Geographic education at that time focused primarily on the presentation of characteristics of different regions of the world, and Minghi (1966: 362) cautioned that "...the political variable, as well as the physical, economic, [and others], is present in any region, and must be given consideration as to its role in influencing the spatial arrangement of things." Minghi criticized excessive reliance on "purely encyclopedic listing and learning" (363) at the expense of conceptual thinking. Instead, he called for the development of an integrated conceptual framework for studying political units, especially nation-states, and its application to world regions and states within them.

In the more than three decades since Minghi wrote, much of what he recommended with such foresight has come to pass. The renaissance of political geography has been closely integrated with the development and application of conceptual frameworks that address such important concepts as the global economy, nationalism and ethnicity, colonialism and post-colonialism, social justice and human rights. Many of the topics that Minghi identified as relevant to a "new" conceptually-oriented political geography—topics such as international relations, the geography of elections, and the partitioning of space for political purposes—remain important research and teaching topics within political geography, as various essays in this volume indicate. In the meantime, political-geographic research has also begun address other topics such as the global environment, the transition to a post-Cold War society and international trade. These new topics are also addressed in this book.

Organization of the Book

The book contains 16 chapters, divided into four parts. Part I including Chapters 2 through 5, examines perspectives on European political geography. In Chapter 2, Brian Blouet examines changes in the political map of Europe that have occurred over the course of the twentieth century. The concept of sovereignty as the primary organizing principle owes its origin to the Peace of Westphalia in 1648, in which the countries of Europe established the sovereignty of states over activities taking place within their borders as a fundamental principle of international law. Frequently, two or more states disputed sovereignty over particular territories. Territorial disputes and resulting wars and conflicts have resulted in numerous changes in the world political map.

The map of Europe was redrawn several times during the twentieth century, especially after World Wars I and II. In this decade alone we have seen the creation of new, independent sovereign states in the former Soviet Union, Yugoslavia, and Czechoslovakia. At the same time, Western Europe is experiencing increasing integration under the auspices of the European Union. In his chapter, Blouet examines these changes and speculates about further changes that might develop in the future.

One of the major historical events affecting the political map of Europe in the twentieth century was the rise and eventual fall of Nazi Germany. In Chapter 3, Colin Flint examines the electoral geography of the rise of the Nazi movement within the Weimar Republic. Why did numerous Germans choose to support a party that engineered the horrible slaughter of millions of Jews and other Europeans while plunging the world into a war that caused the deaths of millions of additional soldiers and civilians? Flint points out that understanding both the spatial and temporal context of the Nazi Party's rise to power is crucial to understanding why the Party won the support it did in elections during the 1920s and 1930s.

Flint's analysis illustrates how conceptual integration is critical to effective teaching of political geography. He argues, using the rise of the Nazis as a case study, that the concepts articulated in Standard 13 and described briefly in this essay cannot be presented or taught in isolation. Rather, it is important that the concepts be presented in an integrative fashion. He points out that the concepts of cooperation and conflict associated with political change can be understood only by considering geographic scale.

Chapters 4 and 5 address the political geography of contemporary changes on the global political map. In Chapter 4, Fiona M. Davidson examines the rise of the European Union and its effects on the political geography of Western Europe. During the Cold War, many in Western Europe argued for increasing economic and political integration, in part to counteract the possible threat of Soviet military activity and territorial expansion. By the mid-1990s, the European Union included 15 members, with others under consideration for future admission.

Davidson's essay focuses on the effects of the development of the European Union on nationalist movements within the European Union's member countries. Throughout Western Europe, national and ethnic groups in places such as Scotland, Wales, Catalonia, and the Basque country of France and Spain have been active in promoting demands for increased autonomy and possible political independence. Davidson examines how the European Union's activities have served to encourage these nationalist movements. The Scottish Nationalist Party (SNP) has enjoyed increasing success at the polls in Scotland in response to its slogan, "Independence Within Europe." As Davidson's essay documents, SNP leaders have argued that Scotland's interests might best be served by political independence coupled with continued membership in the European Union.

In Chapter 5, Stanley Brunn examines changes on the other side of the now-defunct Iron Curtain. Although the Iron Curtain was in reality a line on the map of Europe separating capitalist, democratic Western Europe from communist Eastern Europe, real barriers to spatial interaction—most notably the Cold War—appeared on the European landscape during the more than forty years that the Iron Curtain existed. What has happened to Eastern Europe now that the Iron Curtain is gone? In particular, how has the removal of visible and invisible barriers to spatial interaction affected the lives of people living in communities adjacent to the barriers?

Brunn points out that the removal of barriers to spatial interaction have several different types of effects. These include economic, cultural, social, and many other changes. With the removal of the Iron Curtain, Western goods and cultural practices have flooded across the now-eliminated boundaries. Some communities located on the eastern side of the former Iron Curtain have profited as gateways between West and East. At the same time, some border communities have faced serious problems including smuggling, trafficking in illegal drugs, and organized crime.

Part II of the book, including Chapters 6 through 10, is devoted to issues involving the political geography of the United States. In Chapter 6, Janet Kodras considers the geographic implications of recent changes in the American federal system. The United States, like many other large and ethnically diverse countries, is a federal state. As specified in the Tenth Amendment to the United States Constitution, power is formally shared between the Federal government and those of the fifty states. Although the Tenth Amendment specifies that all powers not specifically delegated to the Federal government formally belong to the states, in practice the division of responsibilities between federal, state, and local governments evolves in ongoing fashion within the United States federal system.

As Kodras points out, the power of the Federal government relative to that of state and local governments expanded during the New Deal period of the 1930s and again in the 1960s. Since the 1970s, the question of federal versus state and local responsibility for various services has been a matter of ongoing political debate within the United States. The election of Republican majorities in both Houses of Congress in November, 1994 was widely interpreted as a mandate to reduce the power of the Federal government. In her essay, Kodras presents a valuable conceptual framework by which students and teachers can examine the variable effects of governmental restructuring on people living in different places across the United States. She then examines how and why changes in national policy have different effects in local places. This framework is useful in helping students learn the political geography of local places within the United States and the relationships between local, national, and global politics.

In Chapter 7, Gerald Webster looks at the question of internal political divisions within the United States. The fifty states of the United States are divided into more than 3,000 counties. In addition, more than 75,000 incorporated municipalities, school districts, special districts and other units constitute local governments in the United States. The proliferation of local governments raises the inevitable question of whether government provision of services will improve with increased centralization.

Will consolidating and centralizing governments make government more efficient? Webster reviews arguments on both sides of this question. Some have argued that centralization makes service provision more efficient and equitable, whereas proponents of decentralization argue that larger units of local government reduce citizen access to public officials. In addition, he argues that larger numbers of governments give citizens more opportunities to choose jurisdiction with higher or lower taxes and service levels. Webster shows how these arguments provide useful opportunities for teachers to initiate learning activities and classroom discussions.

Chapters 8 and 9 examine two important aspects of the electoral process within the United States. In Chapter 8, Jonathan Leib looks at the political geography of the Voting Rights Act. More than thirty years have now elapsed since President Lyndon Johnson signed the original Voting Rights Act into law in 1965, calling this the most significant piece of legislation resulting from the Civil Rights Movement of the 1960s. In his essay, Leib examines the issue of minority voting rights in the United States as affected by the Voting Rights Act. The Act provided that the Federal government would guarantee the rights of African-Americans and other minority group members to vote in Federal, state, and local elections.

Once the Voting Rights Act was implemented, it became evident that the right to vote was of little value to members of minority communities if their residents had no opportunity to elect candidates of their choice to Congress and to state and local legislative offices. The complex and important question arose whether those responsible for drawing electoral district boundaries could or should draw "minority-majority" districts, or districts that contained large numbers of minority residents and would therefore likely elect minority candidates to public office. The question of electoral district boundary delineation is an inherently geographical question. Leib reviews the geographical effects of recent court decisions that addressed this question, and he considers various alternatives to the traditional practice of electing representatives from single-member districts.

In Chapter 9, Douglas Deane Jones examines the contemporary electoral geography of the United States. Electoral geography is the analysis of the distribution of election outcomes across space and over time. These distributions are analyzed in terms of various social, economic, political, and cultural processes. Because formal elections are the primary means by which the United States and other Western democracies resolve disputes over the direction of public policy, electoral geography provides a useful means of teaching the concepts of cooperation and conflict that are so basic to Standard 13.

Jones's essay illustrates the pedagogic value of electoral geography in teaching American political geography. Jones, like Kodras in Chapter 6 and Leib in Chapter 8, points out that the political system of the United States is inherently geographic. He reviews spatial and temporal trends in American presidential elections, the role of geography in campaigns and campaign strategies and the linkage between social movements and electoral geography. Jones concludes with discussion of ideas about how teachers can use these concepts in courses or units on the political geography of the United States.

In Chapter 10, Fred Shelley examines the geography of U.S. foreign policy. Traditionally, scholars of international relations have examined conflicts and alliances between states. The literature has paid little or no attention to differences within states about the conduct of foreign policy. Yet foreign policy in the United States is itself a subject of considerable political debate. Indeed, the political debate over the conduct of foreign policy within the United States is one characterized by substantial geographic regularity, as a result of the varying positions of different sections of the United States relative to the national and world economies.

Foreign policy in the United States, like in other countries, is linked closely to geopolitics. American geopolitics have long been associated with tension between isolationists and supporters of a more active role for the United States within the international system. This tension has by no means been resolved by the end of the Cold War, as debates between isolationists and interventionists have punctuated decisions concerning actual and proposed foreign policy initiatives in Latin America, Europe, Africa, and elsewhere. Shelley's essay illustrates how foreign policy and domestic policy and politics interact with each other using a conceptual framework emphasizing the changing role of the United States within the world economy. He then illustrates how this perspective provides a source of information for teachers and students in political geography.

Part III includes essays that examine problems involving contemporary global and international problems. In Chapter 11, Christopher Merrett investigates the evolution and effects of the recently established North American Free Trade Agreement (NAFTA). Merrett examines whether some regions and economic sectors within North America have stood to benefit from NAFTA at the expense of others. As Merrett points out, the issue of free trade was the subject of vigorous debate within Canada several years before the debate within the United States House of Representatives over the NAFTA authorization bill became front-page news across the United States in 1993.

Focusing on the debate over NAFTA within Canada, Merrett compares the arguments used to support or oppose free trade prior to its implementation with the short- and long-term consequences of the agreement. He uses the Canadian example to provide conclusions about the effects of free trade on national economies. Merrett devotes the final section of his essay to discussion of a role-playing exercise that may be an effective method of teaching free trade. Merrett advocates dividing political geography students into three groups, with students in each group playing the roles of Canadian union workers, American factory owners, and Mexican peasant farmers.

In Chapter 12, William Solecki and Shira Birnbaum look at the political geography of global environmental problems. As everyone knows, industrialization and other changes in the global economy have been associated with important environmental problems, including acid rain, air and water pollution, and the possibility of global warming. Solecki and Birnbaum point out that human-induced environmental change affects both global-scale processes such as global atmospheric and oceanic circulation and local-scale processes such as deforestation, land cover change, and biodiversity loss. Global environmental change has important implications for agricultural production, public health, coastal development, and resource management.

Solecki and Birnbaum argue that global environmental change needs to be examined within the context of local small-scale political conflicts. In that way, the interface between cooperation and conflict inherent in Standard 13 can be applied to environmental conflict. As Solecki and Birnbaum point out, examining global environmental change within the context of local political conflict helps students understand not only the causes of global environmental change but also reasons why society has sometimes failed to address environmental concerns adequately. Students should not view global environmental change as detached from their everyday experience. Rather, they learn how important shifts in the global environment are being played out at the local level through everyday political conflicts. Solecki and Birnbaum include an important directory of teaching resources, including web sites accessible through the Internet. Teachers and students can use these resources to learn more about the political effects of global environmental change.

In Chapter 13, Alice T. M. Rechlin Perkins examines the changing world political map. As she points out, boundaries of social, economic, and cultural regions are fuzzy. Because of the principle of state sovereignty examined by Blouet in Chapter 2, however, political boundaries are abrupt transitions. Reinforcing points made by authors of earlier chapters, Rechlin Perkins illustrates that boundaries on the world's political map at any period reflect the state of cooperation and conflict among peoples of a region at that stage of history.

At the same time, boundaries provide visual images of control over space. Changes in boundaries are often accompanied by changes in place names, flags, and other symbolic manifestations of changes in sovereignty. Efforts and proposals to change place names can meet with opposition, as Rechlin Perkins's example of controversy between Greece and the newly independent former Yugoslav republic of Macedonia illustrates. She illustrates these conflicts with references to various changes in the world political map, including place-name changes that have been implemented during the 1990s. Rechlin Perkins provides a discussion of how the National Geographic Society has been active in revising the Society's *Atlas of the World* in response to these conflicts and changes.

Part IV of the volume is devoted specifically to suggestions for political geography teachers. In Chapter 14, Alice Rechlin Perkins provides a poem as the basis for learning activities about the ever-changing world political map as a follow-up to her Chapter 13. Arlene Shelley discusses the use of writing assignments in political geography classes in Chapter 15. Experts on college and pre-college education have long advocated emphasis on writing to help students learn concepts within the humanities, the natural sciences, and the social sciences. Although the education literature suggests that many college teachers resist efforts to encourage them to require their students to write, Shelly's recent survey of undergraduate geography teachers across the United States revealed that a substantial majority require their students to complete writing assignments. Those teaching courses that involve higher-order conceptual thinking were especially likely to demand writing.

Political geography is a subject that requires students to engage in conceptual thinking. It is not enough to expect political geography students to memorize names, dates, and facts. To develop meaningful understanding of political geography concepts, students must engage in dialogues with each other, with their teachers, and with the subject matter. For this reason, Shelley argues that writing assignments are especially important to teaching political geography as opposed to other types of geography courses. She presents a conceptual framework for the evaluation of effective writing assignments, and then applies this framework to three assignments that have recently been used in political geography classes in the United States.

Finally, Chapter 16, consists of selected learning exercises, presented and edited by Scott R. Myers that teachers can use as a companion piece to Leib's Chapter 8, "Political Geography and Voting Rights in the United States." Teachers can use or develop his case study of U.S. congressional districts in Georgia to illustrate redistricting electoral space. Teachers can also develop or adapt suggestions within the various chapters for classroom use.

References

Archer, J. C., and P. J. Taylor 1981. *Section and Party*. New York: Wiley.

Berry, B. J. L. 1969. "Review of *International Regions and the International System," by Bruce Russet. Geographical Review*, 59: 450-451.

Demko, George J. and William B. Wood 1994. *Reordering the World: Geopolitical Perspectives on the Twenty-first Century*. Boulder, Colorado: Westview.

Geography for Life: National Geography Standards 1994. Washington, D.C.: National Geographic Research and Exploration for the American Geographical Society, Association of American Geographers, National Council for Geographic Education, and the National Geographic Society.

Glassner, Martin Ira 1996. *Political Geography*, 2d. ed. New York: Wiley.

Merrett, Christopher D. 1997. "Research and Teaching in Political Geography: National Standards and the Resurgence of Geography's `Wayward Child'," *Journal of Geography*, 96: 50-54.

Reynolds, D. R., and D. B. Knight 1989. "Political Geography." In *Geography in America*, edited by G. L. Gaile and C. Willmott. Columbus, Ohio: Merrill.

Shelley, F. M., J. C. Archer, F. M. Davidson and S. D. Brunn 1996. *The Political Geography of the United States*. New York: Guilford.

Taylor, Peter J. 1993. *Political Geography: World-Economy, Nation-State and Locality*. New York: Wiley.

Part I: European Perspectives

CHAPTER 2

DIVIDING EARTH SPACE: THE POLITICAL GEOGRAPHY OF EUROPE, 1900-2000

Brian W. Blouet

This chapter is excerpted and adapted from "The Political Geography of Europe: 1900-2000 A.D." by Brian W. Blouet. Used by permission of the *Journal of Geography*, Vol. 95, No. 1 (January/February 1996): 5-14.

"The primary political division of the Earth is by state sovereignty" (*Geography for Life* 1994: 90). States are recognized as sovereign over activities within their borders. States enact laws, issue currency, impose taxes, take censuses, provide services, control cross-border migration, charge tariffs, and conduct foreign policy. In controlling portions of earth space, however, sovereign states can separate themselves from resources, markets and manufacturing capacity outside their borders. International boundaries can be mechanisms that reduce the possibility of economic interaction.

As Standard 11 points out, "Resources are unevenly scattered across the surface of the Earth, and no country has all the resources it needs to survive and grow. Thus each country must trade with others...(85). " The language of this standard implies a world in which the concept of free trade is accepted by all participants.

Over the course of the twentieth century, however, there has not been an easy progression toward the removal of impediments to trade. World War I, World War II, and the Cold War provide examples of efforts to promote conquest of territory on the part of countries making efforts to improve their economic prospects. Both Nazi Germany and the Soviet Union wanted to create autarkic (self-contained) economic systems and thought that territorial expansion would help them to achieve these goals.

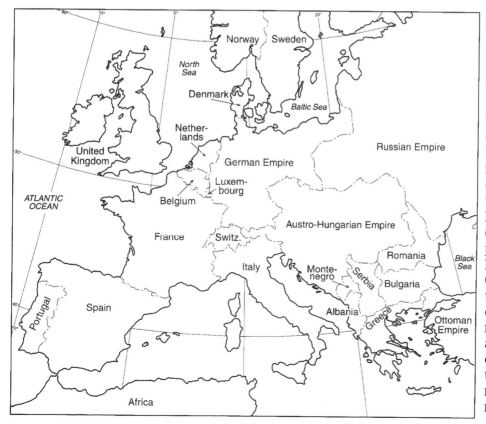

Figure 2.1. Europe prior to WWI

Another way to remove trade barriers is to negotiate away impediments to economic interaction. The states of Western Europe agreed to do this after World War II. The 1957 Treaty of Rome was an attempt to expedite the free movement of goods, capital, and skills through the European Economic Community (EEC). The EEC and its predecessor, the European Coal and Steel Community, can be used to illustrate the idea that countries are better off making resources available to one another on equal terms rather than to try and establish monopolies on raw materials.

Europe, in which the structure of the modern state originated, provides plenty of examples of conflict and cooperation among states. Over the course of the twentieth century, the political map of Europe has been affected by numerous conflicts as well as by various efforts to promote international cooperation. In this chapter, boundary changes resulting from conflict are reviewed along with efforts within Western Europe to produce cooperation among states opening up economic space to one another on equal terms.

The European States Prior to World War I

Prior to the outbreak of World War I, the European state systems were dominated by great powers—Czarist Russia, Austria-Hungary, the Ottoman Empire, Germany, France, and the United Kingdom (Figure 2.1). Europe was a region of competing empires. World War I broke out at Sarajevo, where four of these empires impinged upon each other. Once the war started, it proved impossible to stop it by negotiation. Each contestant struggled to enlarge the territory under its control.

The Chancellor of Germany, for example, spelled out German territorial goals in September, 1914 (Fischer 1967: 103-105). German expansionist policy was focused on its control of *Mitteleuropa*. The term Mitteleuropa refers literally to middle or central Europe, but it also has a broader meaning, carrying the connotation of a region in the heart of Europe within which Germany would be the dominant power, controlling trade and political alignments. Had Germany been victorious in World War I, the German state would have expanded westward at the expense of Belgium and France. In the east, a new tier of German-dominated states would have provided a buffer against Russia (Figure 2.2).

Of course, Germany did not win the war. Britain and France, supported by the United States, forced Germany to capitulate in November, 1918. Instead of a Mitteleuropa dominated by an enlarged German empire, the region was divided into many new states carved out of territory formerly controlled by the Russian, German, and Austro-Hungarian empires (Figure 2.3). These new states included Finland, Estonia, Latvia, Lithuania, Poland, Czechoslovakia, and Yugoslavia. Iceland and the Irish Free State also became independent during this period, while Armenia, Azerbaijan, Georgia, and Ukraine enjoyed brief periods of independence before being absorbed into the Soviet Union.

Many Americans are familiar with President Woodrow Wilson's idea of national self-determination. In the United States, it was assumed that self-determination would create a

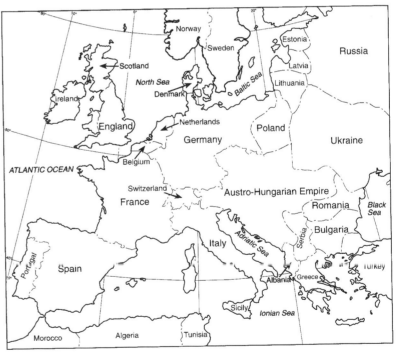

Figure 2.2. Possible states and boundaries in a Post-World War I Europe dominated by Germany

European political map matching nations to states and would promote democracy within Europe. It certainly failed to do that, however, as the new states withheld full rights from minorities and many fell under dictatorial rule. As the new states emerged, most promptly ignored the principle

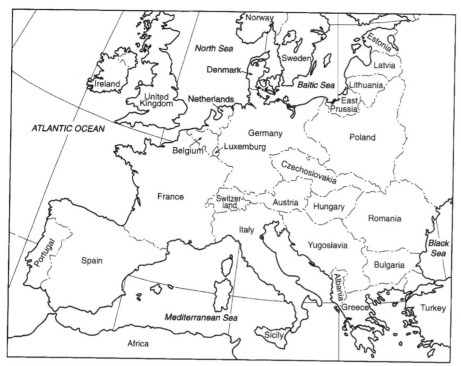

Figure 2.3. Post-World War I Europe

and grabbed as much territory as they could, even if this territory contained members of other national groups.

Not surprisingly, the post-World War I New Europe was unstable and far from being based upon self-determination. One-third of the population of Poland was not Polish. Czechoslovakia contained Hungarians, Germans, and Ruthenians in addition to the Czechs and Slovaks who were not certain they belonged together. Hungary contained German, Slovak, Ruthenian, Romanian, Croatian, and Serb minorities. All of the new states lacked stable political institutions, independent civil services, foreign currency reserves and in many cases central banks. Their sense of instability was aggravated by disputed boundaries.

Germany and the Soviet Union Dominate Europe

The Austro-Hungarian and Ottoman Empires had been broken up after World War I. Germany and Russia, in contrast, re-emerged as great powers in the 1930s.

After the Nazi Party won control of the German government in 1933 (see Chapter 3), Germany began to rearm and expand. Germany remilitarized the Rhineland in 1936, absorbed Austria in 1938, and took over part of Czechoslovakia in 1939. By the late 1930s, the Soviet Union had reappeared as a force in European affairs. Germany and the Soviet Union signed a non-aggression pact on August 23, 1939. They divided Poland, defined spheres of influence in eastern Europe and agreed to increase trade with each other. The Germans saw the pact as securing the German eastern flank, avoiding the possibility of major wars on two fronts. The Soviet Union, meanwhile, was given license to reconquer the old Russian empire in eastern Europe.

Both sides acted on these goals after the pact was signed. The Soviet Union invaded Finland in December, 1939 and in 1940 it occupied Estonia, Latvia, and Lithuania and took territory from Romania. Meanwhile the Germans assaulted Western Europe. In the spring of 1940, Germany occupied the neutral states of Western Europe (Denmark, Norway, Luxembourg, Belgium, and the Netherlands) before defeating France in June.

To dominate all of Western Europe, the Germans needed to defeat Britain. The Royal Navy denied a German invasion fleet passage to Britain, however, and the Royal Air Force controlled the skies above the English Channel. Britain was secure from invasion, but the U.K. and its allies—the former colonies of Canada, New Zealand, Australia, and South Africa—could not put forces back on the continent of Europe. There was stalemate in the West at the end of 1940. The German forces were ordered to the east again in order to widen the European conflict into a two-front war. In the summer of 1941, Germany and her allies attacked Soviet forces along a front that stretched from the Baltic to the Black Sea (Figure 2.4).

Prior to World War II, the states of Central Europe from Sweden to Italy had traded primarily with Germany. During the early and middle years of World War II, trade between Germany and other countries in Central Europe increased. In contrast, Britain had been a more important trading partner with the Western European countries than with Germany. Moreover, Western European countries such as France, Belgium, and the Netherlands maintained extensive oceanic trade with their overseas empires. During the war, however, international trade within Western Europe was directed increasingly toward Germany, altering pre-war trading patterns and establishing trends that were to persist in the postwar world.

Europe after World War II

World War II in Europe ended with the surrender of Germany in May, 1945. The spheres of influence and boundaries of states were redrawn (Figure 2.5).

Eastern Europe passed into the Soviet political and economic orbit. Linkages with West Germany were severed, and international trade patterns were re-oriented to the east on terms dictated by the Soviet Union. The countries of eastern Europe found their pre-war linkages with Germany and the West swept away and replaced by a socialist system. The process of state building in Eastern Europe began all over again behind new boundaries, a new political system, and efforts to rebuild the eco-

Figure 2.4.   The state boundaries of Europe—1942

nomic infrastructure damaged by the war. The eastern part of Germany was severed from the rest of the country and incorporated into the Soviet sphere of influence as the German Democratic Republic or East Germany.

Germany and Western Europe, meanwhile, had suffered widespread devastation during the war. Economic conditions in western Europe got worse during the remainder of 1945 and into 1946. As living standards fell, many feared that communist governments would come to power in western Europe. It was against this backdrop that the United States, which had played a critical role in the defeat of Germany, offered economic assistance to Europe. The American, British, and French sectors of occupied Germany were merged, forming the Federal Republic of Germany. The Russian-occupied eastern sector declined to join the Federal Republic and became the German Democratic Republic under Soviet domination.

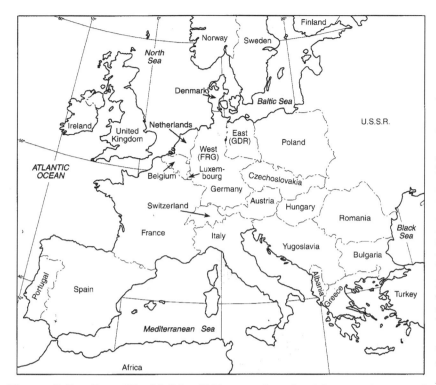

Figure 2.5.   Post-World War II Europe (used with permission of George W. White)

In June 1947, General George Marshall sketched the outline of a plan to help Europe economically. The Marshall Plan helped the European countries rebuild, but it had the effect of dividing the nations of Europe on the basis of economic systems. In July, sixteen European countries met to create the Organization for European Economic Cooperation. The Soviet Union did not attend, however, and pressured the countries of Eastern Europe into declining their invitations. The Soviet response to the Marshall Plan was to create the Council for Mutual Economic Assistance in 1948. Military alliances associated with these organizations came later, with the North Atlantic Treaty Organization established in 1949 and the Warsaw Pact in 1955. Europe was divided into blocs.

A Free Trade Area or a Common Market?

The Organization for European Economic Cooperation, which grew out of the Marshall Plan, can be seen as a step along the road to establishing the European Economic Community (EEC), which today has evolved to become the European Union. The first concrete institution of economic cooperation was the European Coal and Steel Community, established in 1951. This agreement among France, West Germany, Italy, the Netherlands, Belgium, and Luxembourg was designed to remove historical frictions over the resources of the Saar (western Germany), Lorraine (northeastern France), Belgium, and the Ruhr (western Germany) by combining the region's coal, iron, and steel producing capacity within one rationalized framework. Henceforth the coal mines and iron and steel works of Western Europe would be producing for an enlarged market. Coal, iron ore, and steel-making capacity were treated as a west European industrial complex within which state boundaries were of little relevance.

Six years later, the same six states of the European Coal and Steel Community established the EEC. The long-term aim of the EEC was to allow the free movement of goods, capital, and labor among member states. EEC members agreed to remove tariffs on goods from member states, and to establish a common external tariff to be charged on goods entering any member state.

The political basis of the EEC was a rapprochement between France and West Germany. The two countries agreed to relinquish mutual animosities while pursuing long-term national objectives. France would assume political leadership in European affairs, while West Germany would become an economic force in the European Community. Although France and West Germany were the heavyweight countries in the newly formed EEC, it was the smaller countries that could not flourish under a system of protected trade. The Low Countries—Belgium, the Netherlands, and Luxembourg—had established the Benelux customs union in 1947. Antwerp in Belgium and Rotterdam in the Netherlands were European ports, while Luxembourg had a large iron and steel industry that depended on markets beyond that tiny country. The Netherlands were headquarters to trans-national corporations such as Royal Dutch Shell, Unilever, and Philips that needed to operate in an open economic environment. It was the Dutch who in the seventeenth century had pioneered concepts such as free trade and freedom of navigation that have since become the basis of international trade relationships in much of the Western world.

Although the United Kingdom had been a leader in promoting European economic cooperation after the announcement of the Marshall Plan, it did not join the EEC when it was created in 1957. The United Kingdom favored a free-trade model in which countries of Europe should agree to remove all tariffs, dues, duties, and other restrictions on trade in goods originating within the territory of members states. Agricultural products would not be part of the agreement, however, and member states could trade with countries outside the European group on terms of their own choosing. From the perspective of the United Kingdom, the advantage of this scheme was that traditional suppliers of foodstuffs such as Canada, Australia, New Zealand, and South Africa could continue to sell into the United Kingdom market without having EEC tariffs imposed on imports.

In 1959, the United Kingdom and six other countries—Denmark, Sweden, Norway, Switzerland, Austria, and Portugal—founded the European Free Trade Association (EFTA) (Figure 2.6). EFTA members agreed to remove tariffs on goods originating in the territory of other member states but did not impose a common tariff on imports from outside EFTA.

Figure 2.6. The founding members of the European Economic Community (EEC) and the European Free Trade Association (EFTA)

Free Trade Association (EFTA)

During the 1960s, the volume of trade among EEC countries was far larger than the volume of trade among EFTA countries. In the United Kingdom, major manufacturers and financial institutions began to see disadvantages in not being part of the larger European market. In 1972, Britain, Denmark, Norway, and Ireland agreed to join the EEC on January 1, 1973. Norwegian voters rejected the agreement, but the other three entered the EEC. Greece became a member in 1981, and Spain and Portugal followed suit in 1986. At the beginning of 1994, Sweden, Finland, and Austria joined the organization now known as the European Union. Thus the EEC absorbed EFTA: only traditionally neutral Switzerland and Norway, whose voters rejected European Union membership again in 1994, of the original EFTA members were not members of the European Union by the mid-1990s.

Unity and Diversity

How has the increased size of the European Union (EU) affected the political geography of Europe? As the European Union grows in size, some fear that it will become an organization with a centralized administration and a rule book that will stifle national and regional traditions. On the other hand, the EU provides an economic framework within which it may be possible for regions to detach themselves from the jurisdiction of larger states without paying a high economic price. Scotland, for example, is larger in population and contains more resources than several current EU members. If Scotland were to become independent of the United Kingdom, it could remain in the EU, interact economically with the remainder of Europe and not incur the disadvantages suffered by small states in the past. Although there are presently few signs that numerous smaller states will emerge, it is a possible development for the future (see Chapter 4).

Although Western Europe has been marked by a trend toward economic and to some degree political unification, Eastern Europe has moved toward decentralization and disunity. By the late 1980s, it had become clear that the Soviet sphere of influence in Eastern Europe could not be held together. Communist rule in the Soviet Union and the Warsaw Pact countries collapsed. As Brunn indicates in Chapter 5, these changes have had profound effects on the people of Eastern Europe.

These changes affected the political map of Europe yet again. East Germany was absorbed into West Germany, while Eastern Europe and the Soviet Union have been broken into smaller pieces (Figure 2.7). Yugoslavia began to break up into its constituent parts. Slovenia and Croatia broke away in 1991, followed by Bosnia-Hercegovina in 1992, and Macedonia in 1993. At the beginning of 1993, Czechoslovakia dissolved into Slovakia and the Czech Republic.

The Soviet Union attempted to meet changing circumstances by evolving rapidly from an empire into a Commonwealth of Independent States (CIS). Eleven of the fifteen former Soviet republics joined, but four chose full independence. These included Estonia, Latvia, and Lithuania, which had been incorporated forcibly into the Soviet Union in 1940, along with Georgia (which joined the CIS at a later date). Russia has used force, as in the case of Chechnya (a former autonomous socialist republic), to prevent constituent republics within Russia itself from breaking away. Clearly, the process of new state creation has yet to run its course in Eastern Europe and the former Soviet Union.

Figure 2.7. Europe 1994

Conclusion

In 1900, Europe was dominated by large land empires. In the aftermath of World War I, many smaller states appeared. After World War II, an enlarged Soviet empire reappeared as a major force in European affairs. Although Germany attempted to expand its empire before and during World War II, Germany ended the war divided and downsized for the second time in half a century. Fifty years after the war ended, however, Germany has reunified and has emerged as the strongest economy in a Europe that is unifying and submerging national sovereignty in a European Union that has become a major force in world economic affairs.

As the twentieth century draws to a close, Western Europe has seen unification while Eastern Europe has experienced disintegration. Will these trends continue? Some critical questions emerge from this examination of changes in Europe's political geography. Will parts of Eastern Europe—for example Poland, the Czech Republic, Slovakia, and Hungary—become economically and politically integrated into Western Europe?

Will the centrifugal forces in the east continue until so many unstable, nominally independent states emerge that it becomes easy for Russia to reassert control over a broad area? Already in 1996, Russia has persuaded Belarus to give up many of the attributes of an independent state. Within Russia itself, political parties on both the left and the right wing of the political spectrum have called for re-establishment of the old Soviet or Czarist empires. In the West, will the centripetal forces integrating the economic and social policies of EU countries generate a backlash in which countries or regions within countries strive to re-establish national or regional identities?

The answers to the first two questions may depend on Germany. In effect, Germany fought World War I and World War II in order to establish hegemony over *Mitteleuropa*. These ambitions were thwarted, of course, by coalitions of unnatural allies which were brought together to prevent Germany from establishing control of Europe from the Atlantic to the Urals. Since World War II, Germany has been bound into Western Europe by NATO and the EU. But what of Germany's long-standing ambitions in the east? To an extent, these ambitions could be developed in the context of an expanding European Union that includes a new tier of members in eastern Europe.

What happens if instability continues within the former Soviet Union? What is the role of Germany in this case? Will Germany and Russia strike a deal to settle issues in the region lying between them? Before World War II, the Non-Aggression Pact was negotiated with an analogous purpose. Is it possible that continued instability in Eastern Europe will encourage Germany and Russia to negotiate a similar pact today? It is certain that the political map of twenty-first century is one that will be very different than that of the twentieth.

CHAPTER 3

NATIONAL STANDARDS AND NATIONAL SOCIALISM: THE POLITICAL GEOGRAPHY OF THE NAZI PARTY VOTE AND TEACHING TOWARD THE GEOGRAPHY STANDARDS

Colin Flint

At a time when right-wing politicians in Europe, the United States, and Japan are gaining credence and power, it is useful to understand the reasons behind the rise of Adolf Hitler's Nazi (National Socialist German Workers) Party in Germany in the 1930s. Hitler's rule resulted in the deaths of 56 million people, including six million Jews exterminated during the Holocaust and millions of other civilian and military casualties of World War II. A political geography framework can provide unique insights into why enough Germans were attracted to the vile and aggressive message of the Nazi Party to allow the Nazis to seize power following the election of March, 1933.

The political geography approach presented in this paper includes two separate but related concepts: context and geographic scale. These concepts are used to illustrate why Nazism was able to garner significant popular support in Germany between the two world wars. Both the spatial and temporal contexts within which Hitler was able to develop mass appeal are important to understanding the geography of the Nazi party vote. Regional and local differences within Germany also contribute to explaining the distribution of votes for the Nazi Party. Processes operating at the global, state, regional, and local scales are, therefore, all important components of a political geography approach that examines the interaction of these scales and how they combine to form local and regional contexts that influence political behavior.

National Geography Standard 13 emphasizes territorial divisions of the world, geographic scales, and issues of cooperation and conflict. Teachers can introduce the issues of conflicting points of view and self-interest from grades 9 through 12. The integration of these concepts is vital to teaching political geography. To develop fully the teaching of political geography, we should challenge directly any idea of separating these concepts. The identification and separation of the key components of standard 13 are essential as a guide to teaching political geography. Yet understanding the political geography of significant current or past events necessarily involves integration of these key concepts. Students can understand issues of cooperation and conflict associated with political change only by considering geographic scale, as is illustrated in this chapter.

The Nazi Party

The *Nationalsozialistische Deutsche Arbeiterpartei* (National Socialist German Workers or Nazi Party) was founded in 1920 as a revolutionary party with little interest in gaining support through the ballot box (Orlow 1969). After 1924, however, Nazi leaders became increasingly aware that the party's future lay in projecting an image of mass support and achieving power through the electoral process. In the Reichstag or parliamentary election of 1930, the Nazi party won 18.3 percent of the total vote, up from 2.6 percent in 1928 (Orlow 1969). Two years later, the Nazis became Germany's largest party in terms of electoral support by gaining 37.3 percent of the vote. This showing of mass support helped Hitler seize power during the political maneuvering of 1933.

In addition to changing its political tactics, the Nazi party changed the contents of its political message over time in an effort to appeal to particular socio-economic groups in different parts of Germany at different times (Orlow 1969; Stachura 1980). Broadly speaking, the Nazi party's message in the north of Germany was consistently more revolutionary and socialist and targeted to the working classes. In the south, the Nazi message was more nationalistic and targeted to the middle class (Bullock 1980). The Nazi party's ability to project different messages in different places suggests that the party was well aware of the influence of temporal and spatial contexts on the attitudes of the German electorate and the need to address them for generating the maximum vote.

The Global Context for the Rise of Nazism

Scale may be defined by a number of criteria. Political, economic, and social processes operate at different scales. Meanwhile, individuals identify with institutions operating from local to global scales. Households, neighborhoods, and local and national governments are among the structures that we create through our actions and with which we identify. Ultimately, the global scale, however, is the contextual setting of the Nazi Party vote in Weimar Germany, or of any significant political change within a country or region. Although it can be difficult to conceptualize the global scale as a structure with which we can create and identify, it is essential to focus on the important processes operating at the global scale before and during this time and their influences on voter's decisions in Weimar Germany.

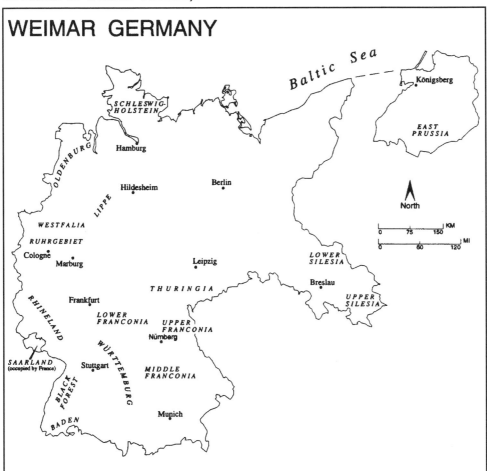

The German Empire was disbanded after its defeat in World War I (Figure 3.1). The Treaty of Versailles required Germany to cede Alsace-Lorraine to France and West Prussia (the Polish Corridor) to newly independent Poland. Representatives from the remaining territories within the new Germany drafted a constitution calling for the establishment of a parliamentary democracy. This constitution took effect in 1919. The *Weimar Republic*, named for the German city in which the constitution was written, enjoyed peace and relative prosperity throughout the 1920s. The Great Depression seriously affected Germany. By

Figure 3.1. Post-World War I Germany: The Weimar Republic

the early 1930s, millions of Germans were unemployed. Disillusionment with democracy as practiced in the Weimar Republic led to the eventual triumph of the Nazi Party and its takeover of the government.

In order to understand the changing geography of the Nazi Party vote in Germany, we must recognize the importance of the global scale and the influences of these scales on voters' decisions in Weimar Germany. The two sets of processes operating at a global scale are economic and political. Over the past several centuries, observers of the world economy have noted the recurrence of Kondriateff waves. Kondriateff waves are periods of economic growth followed by periods of stagnation (Taylor 1993). Generally, a Kondriateff wave lasts approximately fifty years, implying roughly 25 years of growth followed by 25 years of stagnation. Kondriateff waves are analogous to business cycles, but they last longer and occur globally. All countries in the world will experience, to varying degrees, the economic growth or recession characteristic of the period.

The inter-war period was a period of economic recession not only in Weimar Germany but throughout much of Europe, the United States, and other parts of the world. Economic recession was accompanied, in Germany as elsewhere, by mass unemployment, hyper-inflation and more generally a substantial reduction in economic well-being and opportunity for the German people.

The period was also characterized by economic restructuring. During periods of economic restructuring, once-dominant industries in leading economies move to other countries and are replaced by other economic activities. Such is the case in the contemporary United States, where service-sector jobs are replacing manufacturing jobs that are being moved to less developed countries. Areas and populations dependent on once-dominated economic sectors bear the brunt of the recession and its economic consequences. In Weimar Germany, economic restructuring resulted in economic hardship in agriculture, mining, and some sectors of the steel industry. On the other hand, the chemical sector, electronics, and aviation were booming despite nationwide recession (Abraham 1986).

At the global level, the world economy was in a period of hegemonic competition. Derived from the Greek term *hegemon* (leader), hegemony refers to a country that has preponderant economic and political influence in the world. The United States has played this role since World War II, whereas Great Britain was the hegemonic power during the nineteenth century. The period between World War I and World War II, however, was a period in which Britain was losing its power and no one country replaced it. A number of countries, including Germany and the United States, were competing to become the next hegemony.

By playing a role as international banker and manager of Germany's huge reparation payments from World War I, the United States was seen increasingly as being involved directly in the German economy. Between 1924 and 1930, Germany borrowed heavily from other countries, especially the United States (James 1986: 138). America's role in the German economy was challenged by German nationalists, including the Nazi Party. In addition, the global context of economic stagnation and restructuring produced conditions of hyper-inflation and very high unemployment. In July 1922, a United States dollar was worth 493.2 marks, but by November 1923 it was worth 4.2 trillion marks. In December 1923, a quarter of German union workers were unemployed and 47 percent of the remainder were working only half time (Anderson 1945: 103). Although these conditions were ameliorated to some extent during the last half of the 1920s, the global depression of 1930 and 1931 resulted in renewed high unemployment and unpopular deflationary policies.

To summarize, the full name of the Nazi party was the National Socialist German Workers Party. We cannot overemphasize the importance of the first three words. Economic and political processes operating at a global scale created a context in which issues of national competition and the detrimental effects of a crisis in the global economy made nationalist and anti-capitalist political messages appealing. In other words, conflict between states at the global scale produced a context in which the Nazi Party was able to attract mass appeal, or cooperation at the national scale by calling for a united German response against perceived detrimental non-German actors. Thus we have seen the importance of the temporal and spatial context at the global scale in understanding why Nazism became popular. We must consider scales below the state, however, to understand fully the issues of cooperation and conflict in the electoral rise of the Nazi Party.

The Electoral Geography of the Nazi Party Vote

Though economic and political processes operating at the global scale set an overarching context for the appeal of Nazism in Germany, the susceptibility of the German electorate to the Nazi message was not uniform across the different regions of Germany. Variation in levels of support across space in Weimar Germany, as elsewhere, is to be expected because of regional and place-specific contexts. Political geographers have identified these contexts as manifestations of the combined influences of the role of a place in the capitalist world-economy (Agnew 1987), the role of social and political institutions in socializing people into particular political practices, and the consequent sense of place or "collective memory" (Johnston 1991).

The role of a place in the world-economy refers to the economic base of a place or region, what products it produces, how it produces those products, and its level of success in exporting them to other places or regions. The economic well-being of people living in particular places or regions depends on the relationship between these places and the global economy. Issues such as the competitiveness of firms within regions and the demand for their products within the wider world-economy often influences political decisions. This is evident in the contemporary United States, as politicians throughout the country campaign for policies intended to increase the competitiveness of their regions relative to others, or to increase the competitiveness of the United States relative to Japan, the European Union, and other places.

A focus on the institutional framework of a place allows for a detailed examination of the growth and maintenance of institutions that play important roles in political socialization and choices. In conjunction with consideration of the role of place in the world-economy as outlined above, such a focus upon institutions, not only suggests why political behavior varies across space but it also identifies the mechanisms that maintain place-specific norms of behavior. In the case of Weimar Germany, a focus on institutions requires examination of Germany's long history of political fragmentation.

In contrast to other Western European states, Germany was highly fragmented politically until the middle of the nineteenth century. The peace settlement conducted in conjunction with the Congress of Vienna in 1815 after the Napoleonic Wars reorganized the more than 360 medieval German states into a German Confederation consisting of 35 independent states and four free cities. A Federal Diet or legislature was created, but legislation could pass only by unanimous vote of all 39 members of the confederation. Between 1834 and 1888, the German states slowly and in piecemeal fashion joined the *Zollverein* or customs union initiated by Prussia. Although the *Zollverein* facilitated economic integration and cooperation, the German states continued to guard their political independence.

In 1871, the German Empire was formed. Its government included the *Bundesrat* or Federal Council, which was an assembly of ambassadors from the various states, along with a *Reichstag* or Parliament (a popularly elected chamber) symbolizing the unity of the German Empire (Carr 1991). The German Empire persisted until the end of World War I. After the war, the European political map was redrawn (see Chapter 2) and the Weimar Republic was established in what remained of the old German Empire. The old states of Germany became provinces of the Weimar Republic, whose laws could override those of individual states. The legacy of old political, military, religious, and educational institutions in the old states remained, however, producing different norms of political behavior across Weimar Germany. The political evolution of Germany from a patchwork of individual states into a unified state reinforces the expectation that homogeneity of political behavior across Weimar Germany should not be expected.

Rohe (1980) defined the party system of the German Empire as a system of regionally-based *Milieupartien* or parties oriented to local cultures, economies, and events. The different regional social environments and political actors across Germany combined to create a definite and distinctive political regionalism within the Empire. These regional distinctions continued after World War II, shaping political socialization and promoting a particular understanding of the state and its relationship to German society.

Identifying these local milieus helps to explain why Nazi Party support was particularly high in certain areas of the Weimar Republic. For example, traditional anti-republican sentiment fostered Nazi Party support in some areas of Thuringia. Pockets of Protestantism in Catholic-majority Bavaria were locations of high Nazi Party affiliation. In Oldenburg and East Friesland, the highly active and inflammatory speaker Ludwig Munchmeyer helped to facilitate Nazi Party support. Social and political contextual factors such as these lead to an expectation of regionally specific Nazi Party electorates.

We can use two different mapping techniques to examine regional disparities in the strength of

Nazi Party support and the reasons why it differs. The Getis statistic measures the degree of relative clustering of high and low values of a particular variable (Getis and Ord 1992). In our case, we can show which counties of Germany comprise clusters of high-level or low-level support for the Nazi Party, shown for the elections of September 1930 (Figure 3.2) and July 1932 (Figure 3.3). Triangles with their points facing upwards indicate clusters of high levels of support, and triangles pointing downward indicate the clustering of counties with low levels of support. Larger triangles indicate greater degrees of clustering. From Figures 3.2 and 3.3, we can see a broad North-South pattern of Nazi Party support. In particular, eastern East Prussia, the Schleswig-Holstein peninsula, Pomerania, and Lower Silesia were regions of support. Areas of low support can be seen in the Ruhr industrial region and in southern Germany, although clusters of support are found in north Baden and in central and upper Franconia, especially in July 1932 (Flint 1995).

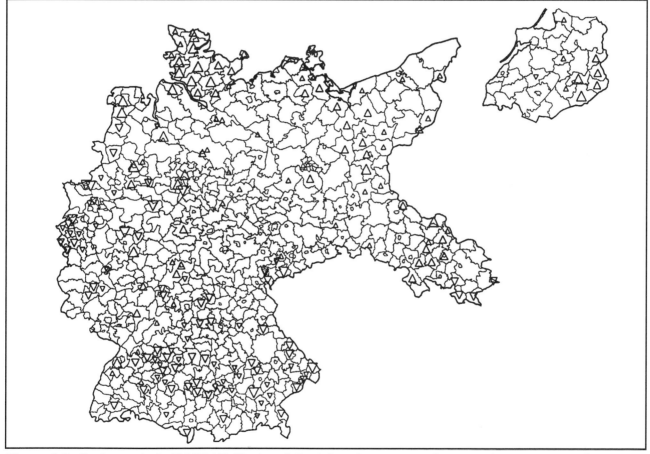

Figure 3.2. Getis statistic-NASDAP (National Socialist German Worker Party) vote, September 1930

Between 1928 and 1930, the areas of greatest change in the Nazi Party vote were eastern East Prussia, Lower Silesia, Pomerania, and parts of Schleswig-Holstein. The areas of smallest change were Bavaria, Wurttemburg, Upper Silesia, the Ruhr, and the Rhineland. We can identify the Nazi Party's electoral support at this critical breakthrough in its rise that occurred in rural areas in northern and eastern Germany. Between 1930 and 1932, in contrast, Nazi support continued to increase in Schleswig-Holstein and Oldenburg. Growth in support flattened out in Lower Silesia and Pomerania, whereas new areas of increased support are seen in Saxony, Hesse-Nassau, and Central and Upper Franconia.

East Prussia is indicative of disparate levels of support for the Nazi Party within the same region. Between both pairs of elections, areas of high growth are bordered by areas of low growth. We can

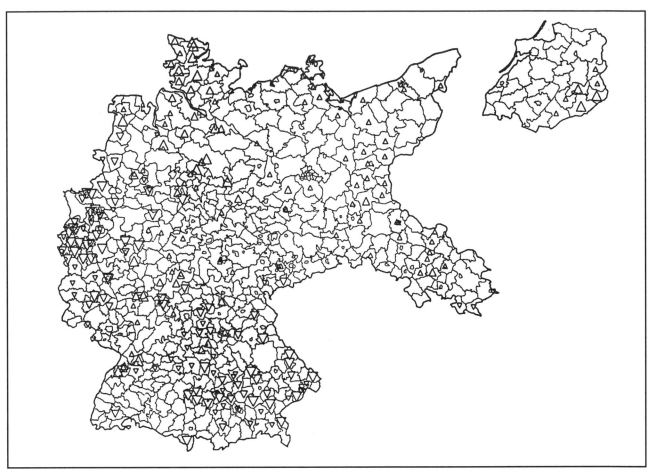

Figure 3.3. Getis statistic-NASDAP (National Socialist German Worker Party) vote, July 1932

also see this pattern in Baden and the Rhineland for both periods. These regions exemplify the claim that patterns of cooperation within the German electorate were formed below the regional scale. Regional patterns of support were aggregations that are likely to include place-specific anomalies. In other words, political behavior in some places was in conflict with dominant regional patterns.

What do these maps say about the interaction of geographic scales and the related issue of cooperation and conflict, as covered by Standard 13? The clustering of high levels of support for the Nazi Party is the geographical expression of cooperation between people, facilitated by proximity and location. As the islands of place specific voting that are in contrast to regional patterns show, cooperation at a regional scale is an aggregation of local behavior that may include places that dissent from a regional pattern.

Summary and Conclusion

Cooperation and conflict involves the construction and interaction of geographic scales. Places cooperated to form regions of support for the Nazi Party, whereas others cooperated to form regions of opposition. Regions of high support are in conflict with regions of low support.

Why are regions of high and low support in conflict with each other? Regional differences in support for political parties result in conflict because power is being sought at a higher scale (the state). Though electoral support is sought within places or regions, parties aim to take control of the state government. Once in power, governments make claims of acting for the state, or in the national interest, whereas their support is often regionally specific. Appeal to the national interest is an artificial claim to cooperation that rarely exists between a country's regions.

Considering cooperation and conflict within a context of interacting geographic scales provides us with another twist, however. As we have seen, economic and political competition between countries was rife in the 1930s as Hitler and the Nazis came to power. Hitler's appeal to the national interest was a call for cooperation within Germany to aid in economic and political conflict between Germany and other states. By appealing to the national interest, the Nazis attempted to subsume regional conflicts that were manifest in their rise to power within a global imperative of competition between countries.

In this chapter, we have examined the myriad of cooperative and conflicting relationships that were part of the Nazi Party's rise to power by using geographic scale as an organizing framework. Starting at the global scale, we understood Hitler's appeal in terms of processes of economic restructuring and hegemonic competition. The differential effects that these processes had upon places within Germany resulted in a geography of support for the Nazi Party. Hitler's message had a varying degree of appeal to the people of Germany, depending on the economic bases of the places in which they lived and place-specific institutions within which voters were socialized. These place-specific patterns of support were amalgamated into regions of strong and weak support for the Nazi Party. The Nazis gained strong support in enough regions to gain control of the country. Once in power, Hitler maintained a confrontational attitude toward other countries while crushing internal opposition by making claims to the national interest.

By going up and then down a hierarchy of geographical scales, we have created a contextual framework that helps us to understand how and why the Nazi Party came to power. In addition, we have seen the complexity of political relationships between the people of one country—the simultaneous geographical expression of political cooperation and conflict. These simultaneous expressions of cooperation and conflict exist because people experience economic and political processes in places, must organize within places and regions to gain political strength, aim to gain control of the national government, and are citizens of countries competing against one another.

Learning Activities

Geographic scale is evident in the overlapping expressions of political cooperation and conflict. Although we have examined this relationship between cooperation and conflict and geographical scales in the extreme case of the rise of the Nazi Party, we can apply a similar framework to other political activities. In this way, we can apply the central components of Standard 13 to any conflict situation at any scale.

The following list of questions might form the basis of learning exercises to encourage students to develop these relationships:

1. What issues and concerns to people have that they consider political?
2. Which of these concerns are likely to be shared by other people living in the same household? In the same neighborhood? In the same city or town? In the same region? In the same country? In the world?
3. At each of these scales, if we achieve consensus upon a political issue with what other scales will conflict ensue?
4. How has the economic role of your town or city changed in the past 100 years? How have these developments changed its relationships with neighboring towns and cities? How have these developments affected its relationships with places outside the United States?
5. Have the effects of these changes been uniform across your neighborhood, city or town, or region? Have they had different effects on different socioeconomic, demographic, or ethnic groups?
6. How have these changes and their effects been reflected in political discussion and competition? Are these concerns at odds with other concerns in the region, or in other regions? How do politicians representing your town or city talk about the relationship between it

and the rest of the world? Does this differ between politicians that are elected to local office and those elected to Congress and other national offices?

References

Abraham, D. 1986. *The Collapse of the Weimar Republic.* New York: Holmes and Meier.

Agnew, J. A. 1987. *Place and Politics: The Geographical Mediation of State and Society.* Boston: Allen and Unwin.

Anderson, E. 1945. *Hammer or Anvil: The Story of the German Working-Class Movement.* London: Victor Gollancz.

Bullock, A. 1992. *Hitler and Stalin: Parallel Lives.* New York: Knopf.

Carr, W. 1991. *A History of Germany,* 1815-1900. 4th ed. New York: Edward Arnold.

Flint, C. 1995. "The Political Geography of Nazism: The Spatial Diffusion of the Nazi Party Vote in Weimar Germany." Unpublished Ph.D. dissertation, Department of Geography, University of Colorado at Boulder.

Getis, A., and J. K. Ord 1982. "The Analysis of Spatial Association by Use of Distance Statistics," *Geographical Analysis,* 24: 189-206

James, H. 1986. *The German Slump: Politics and Economics,* 1924-1936. Oxford: Clarendon.

Johnston, R. J. 1991. *A Question of Place.* Oxford: Basil Blackwell.

O'Loughlin, J., C. Flint and M. Shin 1995. "Regions and Milieux in Weimar Germany: The Nazi Party Vote of 1930 in Geographic Perspective," *Erdkunde,* forthcoming.

Orlow, D. 1969. *The History of the Nazi Party,* 1919-1933. Pittsburgh: University of Pittsburgh Press.

Rohe, K. 1990. "German Elections and Party Systems in Historical and Regional Perspective: An Introduction." Pp. 1-25 in *Elections, Parties and Political Traditions,* edited by K. Rohe. New York: Berg.

Stachura, P. D. 1980. "The Political Strategy of the Nazi Party, 1919-1933," *German Studies Review,* 3: 261-288.

Taylor, P. J. 1993. *Political Geography: World Economy, Nation-State and Locality* 3d edition. New York: Wiley.

CHAPTER 4
A NEW EUROPE? THE EUROPEAN UNION AND THE REGIONS: THE CASE OF SCOTLAND
Fiona M. Davidson

> "We are bought and sold for English gold
> Such a parcel o' rogues in a nation"
> A. Burns

These lines summed up Burns's view of the Scottish parliamentarians who signed the Act of Union in 1707. Since Burns wrote them only eighty years after the Act was signed, one might assume that his venom was a consequence of the very recent trials and turmoils that the Union had wrought upon Scotland, most notably in the 1715 and 1745 Jacobite risings. Today, however, it has become clear that 2007 will bring no celebration of the Tercentenary of the Act (whatever the state of the Union twelve years hence). Generations later, Scots again share Burns's distaste and anger at this shotgun marriage, and simultaneously across Europe other peoples, similarly coaxed, coerced, bribed, or forced into accepting alien sovereignty are expressing their desire if not for outright independence, at least for a greater voice in their own destiny.

This sudden surge in separatist sentiment has come to Western Europe at the same time as the continent is experiencing the greatest drive towards unification since the Roman Empire and the twin forces of integration and disintegration are creating a situation of increasing stress for national governments. It may seem paradoxical that Europeans are simultaneously promoting integration at one spatial level and disintegration at another. This is no paradox, only the potential development of a new form of political organization of space. Just as Europe gave the world the European State Model, a centralized, autonomous, national power with fixed boundaries and a determination to create national loyalty and a national culture based on the majority ethnic population—so Europe may now be moving beyond the nation-state to a two-tier form of political organization (Davidson 1997).

The trigger for this change has been the development of the global economy. Just as economics was the driving force behind the integration and creation of the European state, so the reorganization of the world economy is removing the *raison d'être* for these same states and is creating an entirely new political playing field, on which these small national and regional units can play just as effectively as the larger states.

These changes have not yet been reflected in the formal political structure of Europe in terms of boundaries. The growth of regional institutions, both those indigenous to the regions and those sponsored by the European Union (EU), is creating a web of trans-regional, multi-regional, and inter-regional political and economic links that is completely bypassing the traditional national governments (Murphy 1993; Keating 1995; Rhodes 1996). The increasing political maturity and sophistication of regional politicians and institutions and the increasingly direct linkages between the regions and the European Union provide both confidence for the regions and a sense of the declining relevance of national political institutions. This paper examines the effects of these economic and political changes on the United Kingdom, with specific reference to increasing demands for regional autonomy emanating from Scotland.

The Act of Union and Scotland's Integration into the British Economy

The question of whether Scotland was an active or reluctant partner in the Act of Union has been debated by historians *ad nauseam*. Nonetheless, few salient facts suggest significant economic coercion involved in the process. The Navigation Acts passed by the English parliament in the 1660s brought legal trade to and from Scotland to a virtual standstill in the late seventeenth century. These acts required that all trade from English colonies be carried to English ports in English ships and this constriction on Scottish trade (which was largely to and from the English controlled American colonies) led to the financially and psychologically disastrous attempt to create a

Scottish colony in the New World—the Darien expedition of 1696. The failure of this venture is estimated to have stripped Scotland of approximately one third of her accumulated financial reserves and was followed up by the East India Company's confiscation of all the remaining ships of the Company of Scotland, rendering overseas trade impossible. By 1706 it was a simple matter for the English parliament to threaten trade sanctions every time the Scottish parliament stepped out of line. Deprived of the ability to make any decisions that would adversely affect England, it became clear, at least to the land-owning class, that an amalgamation of the parliaments was the only solution. Any parliamentary opposition was fictionalized and quickly silenced by a reparations grant of almost 400,000 British pounds. Popular discontent, so well expressed by Burns, was easily ignored at a time when the franchise was limited and only a minority of male citizens had the right to vote.

Opened to trade with England and the colonies, Scotland began to thrive economically, and the boom continued with the growth of the industrial revolution. It was clear that the larger economy created by the Act of Union, with further expansion through the acquisition of Empire, created an economically beneficial situation for both Scotland and England. With a large, stable, prosperous market, ample supplies of both domestic and imperial raw materials, more than adequate capital, innovation, and entrepreneurship, the new Great Britain was set to become the industrial powerhouse of the world for four or five generations. With full employment, a booming middle class and emigration opportunities for the discontented, no one questioned the wisdom of having submitted to a reduced voice in self-determination. As is frequently the case, economic satisfaction bred political satisfaction.

Even with the fall of Empire, the Commonwealth links and, throughout the 1950s and 1960s the lack of alternate trade links, made a disintegration of the Union a dream for only the most ardent Scottish nationalists. The turning point was to come in 1973, in two separate and quite unrelated incidents. The most immediately important, although ultimately less so, was the discovery of oil in the North Sea. Much of the oil discovered in the 1960s was found in what would be considered Scottish territorial waters. With the oil price increases of the 1970s and the desire to reduce the Western world's dependence on OPEC oil, it appeared that Scotland could support an economic claim to be independent. Thus in the 1970s the battle cry of the newly revitalized Scottish National Party (SNP) was "It's Scotland's Oil."

At the same time, an event that was to prove much more important to Scotland's search for self-determination had taken place. On January 1, 1973 the United Kingdom finally joined the European Economic Community (EEC), the forerunner of today's European Union. Once the United Kingdom joined the EEC, economic ties to the Commonwealth were gradually weakened and in many cases cut completely. This greatly reduced the economic advantages of being tied to England. Instead, it became advantageous to be linked with the EEC—a goal places like Scotland could, in theory at least, achieve independently of the United Kingdom.

During the 1970s and early 1980s, the EEC was in serious economic and political trouble bogged down in fights over regulation, rebates, and subsidies. The EEC was not yet a major force in world trade. Without a secure framework for international trade, hopes of getting popular support for independence were in vain. By the 1990s, however, a stronger and more prosperous organization, by now known as the European Union, emerged as a major player on the world's economic stage. With the strengthening of the European Union came renewed efforts within Scotland and other regions with strong nationalist movements to press for independence. Recognizing this possibility, the SNP adopted the slogan of "Independence in Europe." This slogan typifies the revitalization of the European ideal, in particular the huge expansion of economic and political integration that has taken place since the mid-1980s that has given nationalist and separatist parties across Europe the confidence to press their claims for self-determination (Davidson 1996).

The Expansion of Economic Integration in Europe in the 1980s

By the early 1990s, leaders of the EU had set as a goal the removal of remaining barriers to the flow of capital, goods, services, and people within the EU's member states. This goal had the active support of much of Europe's business community although many politicians opposed it. Neither of these reactions was unexpected. Politicians were well aware that any increase in the power of the EU was a potential threat to the individual sovereignty of each member state. Business leaders in Europe believed that economic integration could only improve Europe's competitive position in the world economy, if for no other reason than the removal of costs associated with intra-European business transactions.

The EU developed the Cockfield Plan to create a single market in Europe. The Cockfield Plan addressed such issues as industrial standards, farm subsidies, uniform visa requirements, and standardized minimum wages. Although much of the plan was modified or delayed as politicians argued over the speed and extent of economic unification, the plan was substantially pushed forward during the economic recovery of the late 1980s and much of it is in place today.

The Cockfield Plan not only encouraged economic and physical integration but it also expanded the political scope of the EU, specifically with reference to regional issues. Regional development is no longer the sole prerogative of national governments. The European Regional Development Board was specifically designed to use *Structural Funds* to support job creation, infrastructure development and improvement, education, training, cultural development, and restructuring assistance to regions within the community. Although funds cover a maximum of 50 percent of the cost of a project and must be matched by regional or national government funds, the Structural Funds come from an agency that has quite different priorities and prejudices than do many of the national governments. This is extremely important in depressed or disadvantaged regions that may perceive that the national government does not have their best interests at heart.

The European Union also encourages regionalism in more direct ways. The 1992 Treaty of Maastricht, which provided a blueprint for the eventual political unification of Europe, required that the *principle of subsidiarity* be applied in all EU decision-making processes. Subsidiarity implies that any decision be taken at the lowest possible level of public domain. Higher levels of government should only act when lower levels cannot do so satisfactorily. In principle this will shift a great deal of power from national governments to the appropriate local and regional governments.

In addition, since the mid-1980s the EU has encouraged politicians from regional parliaments to meet and cooperate on economic, cultural, and environmental issues. The *Committee des Regions* is specifically designed as a forum for regional politicians to meet, cooperate, and influence EU legislation that pertains to regional concerns. The EU also provides support for a host of regional organizations, including the Atlantic Group, Interreg, the Conference of Peripheral Maritime Regions, the Assembly of European Regions, the Consultative Committee of Regional and Local Authorities, and the Euroregion project, among others, providing funds, support, and political legitimacy to non-national groups.

The European Union and Scotland
The European Union functions as a collective body of its fifteen national state governments. The representatives of those governments make decisions, remit funds to the EU, and receive funds from the EU through their respective national treasuries. As a constituent part of the United Kingdom rather than a sovereign state, Scotland has no independent bargaining voice within the EU. This leads to a situation in which the interests and needs of the Scottish economy tend to be overlooked in the broader context of the needs of the United Kingdom economy with its southeastern focus.

The lack of adequate public accounting in the United Kingdom has created the suspicion that EU *rules of additionality* are not being adhered to. The EU requires that all EU grants be *added* to the public expenditures of a country rather than substituted for internally generated revenues. At the national level in the United Kingdom it is impossible to trace EU money once it enters the treasury. It is therefore impossible to guarantee additionality. A greater degree of accountability operates at the regional level. All of Scotland's EU money is administered through the Scottish Office. From there money is allocated to the regional councils and to individual projects. At this level all the money is used for Scottish projects. The Scottish Office currently has the authority to negotiate directly with the EU on certain projects, although the money must still pass through the Treasury of the United Kingdom in Westminster.

At the same time, it must be remembered that the Scottish Office is just another arm of the United Kingdom. It is not a representative body for Scotland, and for the last seventeen years has been an outpost of English Conservative thinking in an overwhelmingly Labour voting population. The decisions of the Scottish Office are linked much more closely to policy directives from Westminster than they are to the needs of the Scottish economy. Nevertheless, the Scottish Office has exercised some independent thinking in lobbying for EU money, with the result that most of Scotland has been classified as eligible for structural fund assistance and Scotland has a relatively high per capita allocation of such funds (although this also reflects the existing poor state of the Scottish economy) compared with England. Autonomous action on the part of the Scottish Office is permitted only at the pleasure of Her Majesty's Government. As one of the most centralized governments in Europe, Westminster is free to rein in the Scottish Office at any time. Should Scotland be perceived to be benefiting too much from their more flexible links with the European Union, this would not be an unlikely scenario.

How much has Scotland benefited from the EU? Looking at the disbursement of funds since the late 1980s it is clear that many projects, both completed and ongoing, would not have been possible without the EU. Leaving aside the issue of whether public expenditure from Westminster is being cut back because of this inflow of EU money, the direct economic benefit of the structural funds since 1988 has been significant. Between 1988 and 1993, $588.8 million was disbursed in the Strathclyde (Glasgow) region. Strathclyde is classified as an Objective 2 region, that is a region suffering from industrial and urban decline, with high unemployment, low income, and structural weaknesses in the economy. The grants are funneled through a variety of programs and come from the European Regional Development Fund and the European Social Fund. At the regional level these funds are coordinated through the Strathclyde Integrated Development Office, which is charged with arranging local and national matching contributions, coordinates and oversees the direction of the project with the grant recipient, and prepares the annual and bi-annual reports on progress for the EU. To date the funds have been targeted towards a variety of different projects, including the promotion of innovation and investment, environmental cleanup, providing industrial sites, providing vocational training, improving transportation, promoting tourism, and upgrading sanitation infrastructure.

Effects of the EU on the Scottish National Party

It has not escaped the attention of the Scottish National Party (SNP) that Scotland's participation in the newly emerging European Union is heavily curtailed and biased by the Westminster influence. Not only are Scotland's priorities overlooked or even ignored when Westminster bargains with the EU, but Scotland also suffers the stigma of being associated with the Conservative party's strong anti-European stance. Neither has the party failed to notice that the newly revitalized EU would provide a very satisfactory framework for economic and political security in the event of Scotland's achieving independence.

The SNP's stance is that the EU now provides the economic links to the global economy that the UK provided, and the union has become obsolete, from an economic perspective. In effect the UK government is too small to provide an adequate framework for international trade in the 1990s, but at the same time it is too large to manage more local levels of government with any degree of sensitivity. This theme that has been played out again and again in Western Europe in the last two decades and has contributed to the formation of regional parliaments in Spain and Belgium.

The SNP uses the idea of economic stability in the EU as a campaigning strategy to reduce the understandably high level of fear and uncertainty that plagues the Scottish population every time they seriously consider independence. A measure of that fear can be gauged from responses to survey questions about independence. When a survey for *The Scotsman* newspaper asked: "If Scotland should separate completely from England?" only 26 percent of the respondents said "Yes." The same question posed by the SNP and phrased rather differently as "Do you think Scotland should be an independent member of the European Union?" drew a 58 percent favorable response.

It appears that the message is slowly getting through. Scotland will not be alone in the world if she chooses independence. Electoral support for the SNP is slowly beginning to reflect this realization. In the 1980s, the SNP came in third or fourth in most elections for seats in Parliament. In the vast majority of elections, SNP candidates won less than 15 percent of the vote. By the 1990s, however, the SNP had become Scotland's second party after Labour, with support in national elections at 26 percent and in local elections at 30-40 percent. In 1997, for example, the SNP ran second to Labour, and the third-place Conservatives failed to win a single seat in Parliament. Public opinion polls indicate 30 percent support for independence, with an additional 40 percent of the population supporting some form of constitutional change that grants greater local autonomy to Scotland.

Conclusion

Of all the states in Europe in which separatist tendencies were likely to emerge, the United Kingdom, Belgium, and Spain have the most active regional movements. Nonetheless, other groups are actively working towards regional autonomy in both Italy (north and south) and France. For all these regional groups the strengthening of the EU has provided and continues to provide both direct and indirect support for their aims. The simultaneous redistribution of power to the EU and the regions and away from the national governments will continue in the foreseeable future. It is possible that the future will bring a Europe in which the national governments are effectively obsolete, with their global functions (defense, trade, economic planning) handled by the EU, and their local functions (education, health care, social services) handled by regional governments. Whether the European State can then resist the centrifugal forces inherent in any multi-ethnic state (and the majority of European states are multi-ethnic) and maintain its physical integrity remains to be seen.

Like all states, the United Kingdom should not be regarded as a fixed entity. The United Kingdom was created by the Act of Union in 1707. It expanded in 1801 to include Ireland, contracted in 1921 when the Republic of Ireland became independent, and may have to change again to accommodate a political solution to the problem of Northern Ireland. There is no reason to suppose that the boundaries of the United Kingdom, or of any state, are immutable. The last decade has brought a number of major changes to the world political map, and, as the distribution of political power changes in Europe, we should expect to see these changes continue.

References

Davidson, F. M. 1996. "The Fall and Rise of the SNP since 1983: Analysis of a Regional Party," *Scottish Geographical Magazine*, 112: 11-19.

_____1997. "Integration and Disintegration: A Political Geography of the European Union, *Journal of Geography*, 96: 69-75.

Keating, M. ed. 1995. *The European Union and Regions.* Oxford: Oxford University Press.

Murphy, A. B. 1993. "Emerging Regional Linkages within the European Community: Challenging the Dominance of the State," *Tijdschrift voor Economische en Sociale Geografie*, 84: 103-118.

Rhodes, M. 1996. The Regions and the New Europe. Manchester, U.K.: Manchester University Press.

CHAPTER 5

WHEN WALLS COME DOWN AND BORDERS OPEN: NEW GEOPOLITICAL WORLDS AT THE GRASSROOTS IN EASTERN EUROPE

Stanley D. Brunn

The world political map contains nearly two hundred states. These states are delimited by boundaries, some of which have been recognized for centuries, whereas others are new creations. Boundaries run the gamut from being highly impermeable to being free and open to the movement of goods, people, and ideas. Moreover, the boundaries themselves are dynamic (Taylor 1994). Some of the dynamism is the result of political and social events within states, whereas other boundaries change in response to events in adjacent states or in the world's major powers (Johnston and Taylor 1989; Demko and Wood 1994; Kegley and Raymond 1994).

What happens when boundaries change? How are people's lives and their economies and communities affected? This chapter will address these questions as applied to eastern Europe following the end of the Cold War. These questions fit within the rubric of a humanistic political geography, which looks at identities, images, and allegiances toward political spaces. Many of these topics could also be addressed in other regions in which boundaries have different meanings and in which states themselves have experienced substantial internal change, for example, in the former Soviet Union, Israel and Palestine, South Africa, Cuba, Vietnam, and China.

Border Landscapes

The border landscapes of the world—places located near international boundaries—are marked by series of observable markers that identify territory. The appearance and significance of border landscapes change in accordance with improved or worsening global and regional political developments.

Border landscapes are human creations. They include not only the borders themselves but also nearby communities and institutions whose activities are influenced by the presence of the boundary. Some borders are marked merely by signs whereas others are heavily fortified. Some are plain and inconspicuous, and others are elaborate. Some are unfortified, and others are marked by armed guards, security forces, dogs, or electric fences. Traffic across boundaries may be light or heavy. Some are open borders across which travelers are welcomed. Others are closed, and forbid or discourage people from crossing.

Boundary markers and border landscapes change in accordance with watershed events in history. Fences that had been erected in order to impede or eliminate cross-boundary interaction, for example the Berlin Wall, may be removed once the rationale for constructing them no longer exists. The decision to erect or to remove a barrier to interaction along a boundary is one made within a state itself. Barriers may be erected to ensure that outsiders, consumer products, and ideas remain outside, or they may be built to keep people in and preclude them from moving to states beyond where greater freedom of mobility and expression may exist. In the same way, states themselves decide when to lower or remove barriers, whether they be imposing physical barriers or legal restrictions to economic and social interaction.

When a state or a group of states makes decisions about removing walls or fences, these decisions become major news events. A decision to remove a wall or fence is a decision to encourage increased interaction across a border landscape. Such decisions reflect changing state policies concerning spaces, peoples, communities, and economies enclosed by the walls, as well as those living and working outside or beyond them. The immediate effects of such decisions on neighboring states is likely to include exchanges of diplomats, visits by delegations of high-level dignitaries, and meetings with international organizations including those that fund new development projects, promote human rights, or assist in drafting new constitutions. These exchanges are often accompanied by visits by sports teams, cultural groups, educators and students, journalists, tourists, and former citizens who voluntarily or forcibly left decades earlier.

The removal of a barrier also affects the day-to-day lives of people in communities near boundaries. Changes in economic livelihood, personal mobility, community activities, and social organization at a local level may not be headline items on national or global television or in major world newspapers. Nevertheless, they represent significant developments within these communities and in the daily lives of citizens. What does the removal of a fence or border post mean? What does it mean for the states separated by these barriers, and for those living along the boundaries? First, the disappearance or reduction of a barrier as an image of intimidation represents openness. A more open border increases the amount of movement across the boundary. Second, the removal of the barrier signifies a change in interstate relations. A state that had formerly restricted movement has adopted a change in policy that legitimizes movement. Legitimized increases in movement mean that a once-closed state must begin to cope with new forms of commerce and ideas, not only for its own citizens but also for those outsiders now entering the state to open it to new consumer products, investments, travel, and other activities.

Worlds without Walls in Eastern Europe

In 1946, Sir Winston Churchill noted that an "Iron Curtain" had descended across the continent of Europe (Taylor 1990). For more than four decades, borders between Soviet-dominated Eastern Europe and the West were closed and difficult to permeate. The Iron Curtain collapsed, however, in the late 1980s. One by one, the countries of eastern Europe replaced their Soviet-dominated governments with democracies. The collapse of Communism in Eastern Europe and the Soviet Union ended nearly half a century of border landscapes characterized by high walls and fences (Kegley and Raymond 1994; Agnew and Corbridge 1995).

How has the removal of these walls affected life near the boundaries of the countries of Eastern Europe? How have the lives of residents of the many small and unnamed villages along boundaries such as those between Austria and the Czech Republic, Austria and Slovakia, Italy and Slovenia, and Slovenia and Hungary been affected by these startling developments? Those who lived near the fences, barricades, and other landscapes of intimidation, fear, and military force are most aware of what the local geographies were like during the Cold War, when cross-boundary interaction was limited severely.

Older residents remember the landscapes as they existed before the Iron Curtain descended. Once the boundaries were closed, these persons learned how fences stifled interaction. They learned that they could no longer communicate officially with friends and relatives across the border. Shopkeepers learned that the barriers defined clearly what goods they could peddle, what currency they could use and where their customers came from.

Boundaries were sometimes used to influence intellectual activity as well. In some states, the flow of ideas was restricted by regulations governing what people could read in newspapers or magazines, where they could travel, and with whom they could communicate. Those living in states where there was more freedom of travel, expression, and purchasing goods knew that citizens of imprisoned spaces across the border had different lives, economics, political choices, and citizen rights.

Today, the removal of the barriers associated with the Iron Curtain has had profound effects in the lives of Europeans who have lived and worked near the once-formidable boundaries between states of the East and West. Numerous changes are evident in the small border communities. The extent to which these changes affect the lives of individuals will depend on several factors, including the community's proximity to the border and the previous permeability of the boundary. We can identify several types of changes affecting day-to-day life in border communities. These include new economic landscapes, new social landscapes, new political landscapes, and new personal landscapes.

New Economic Landscapes

The boundaries between Eastern and Western Europe were impermeable in large measure because they reflected profound differences in economic philosophy. As Chapter 2 in this volume demonstrates, Eastern Europe was part of an *autarkic* system of centrally planned economies dominated by the Soviet Union while the economies of the West were more oriented to free trade. Not surprisingly, the removal of economic restrictions in Eastern Europe had especially significant effects near the borders.

The removal of the borders has created new markets for goods from Western Europe and the United States. Western-based multinational corporations see new markets in Eastern Europe for their products and services. European and American goods including cassette tapes, cosmetics, blue jeans and other Western clothing, souvenirs, videotapes, magazines, and other consumer items are now available in large department stores, smaller shops, outdoor markets, and roadside stands. Merchants and customers travel long distances to buy and sell Western consumer products at trade fairs, arriving in buses, minivans, trucks, and cars of all sizes, shapes, and conditions imaginable. Even a cursory examination of the license plates of these vehicles, the languages spoken, and the dress of buyers and sellers reveals a startling array of old and new cultures.

Advertising is now common in countries where it once was prohibited. Goods and services are advertised on storefronts, free-standing billboards, and the sides and tops of buildings. Advertising means competition as well as product differentiation. Consumers respond to advertising by seeking individual advantages in making their purchases. The English language is now part of the advertising landscape. English is used in product names, slogans, and sponsoring television programs.

Many cities on both sides of once-closed borders are now experiencing gateway functions. Vienna and Trieste are good examples of Central European cities that were once considered peripheral to the European economy, but now find themselves serving as gateways to eastern and southeastern Europe. Smaller cities and towns near international borders serve similar functions on a smaller scale.

The commercial faces of these rural settlements also reflect the changing political landscape. Not only do private shops sell Western goods, but consumers can now patronize fitness clubs, discotheques, and casinos. Credit and debt are now acceptable, and VISA and EUROCARD signs appear on many storefronts to attract shoppers. Shops to exchange currency and send faxes, tourist offices, campgrounds, recreation areas, real estate agencies offering property to outsiders, private physicians and therapists, and other businesses have been established in many border towns. Western-style fast food restaurants such as McDonald's, Pizza Hut, and Kentucky Fried Chicken are popular, albeit very expensive. Downtown areas have been renovated, with commercial strips developed. Bright colors and attractive signs promote private enterprise, which are profiting at the expense of the old state-run stores.

New Social Landscapes

The social and cultural landscapes have also changed with open borders. Persons can now visit friends and relatives across the border. Those on either side of the boundary are free to attend weddings, baptisms, funerals, family reunions, and other ceremonies. Churches, parks, historical monuments, and other places once tightly controlled by police states are now open to the public. Museums are displaying new exhibits on previously prohibited topics. Citizens can now see military and industrial landscapes, including areas of extreme environmental deterioration once closed to travelers. Village festivals celebrated by those of common heritage are attended by persons on both sides of border. School children, business leaders, local government officials, and merchants can now explore new worlds with those residing in close proximity.

Open borders have revolutionized communication. Mail, packages, faxes, and electronic mail can now be sent across spaces once separated by bureaucratic and ideological barriers. Libraries now received once-banned books and magazines, and librarians are confronted with demands for access to previously censored state materials. Movie theaters show the latest films from Hollywood and elsewhere. Television and radio frequencies are no longer jammed, demonstrating that popular access to the mass media is no longer controlled by the state. Journalists now cover stories about topics and events that they never could previously.

Sports have become a promoter of regional cooperation. New sports, new leagues, and new teams have appeared. National teams include players, coaches, trainers, and sponsors from the West along with Western-made uniforms and equipment. Talented athletes from the eastern side of the Iron Curtain, such as National Basketball Association stars Toni Kukoc, Arvydas Sabonis, and Dino Radja and National Hockey Associations Sergei Federov and Jaromir Jagr have signed lucrative contracts with professional teams from Western Europe and North America.

New groups from Western Europe and the United States have appeared on the scene. These groups include teachers of English, activists working to protect environmentally sensitive areas, persons introducing Western cultural innovations such as baseball, Peace Corps volunteers working to promote rural development or technological innovation in education and health care, and missionaries representing American evangelical denominations. Non-government organizations (NGOs) and voluntary groups see vast opportunities for growth in these newly opened border areas, and each carves out new administrative spaces for their activities.

Not all cross-boundary traffic across the newly opened border is welcome. Residents of states and communities near the borders may welcome tourists and investment bankers, but they do not welcome expatriates who buy up local land and businesses, refugees, ethnic minorities, smugglers, prostitutes, drug traffickers, and those peddling conventional and nuclear weapons and stolen property. It is not surprising that national mafias (extra-legal and often organized-crime groups) have emerged in the spirit of incipient and creative capitalism. Some of these new national mafias are connected to extensive and sophisticated continental and global networks. Some are engaged in banking and money laundering, others in weapons sales or international terrorism.

New Political Landscapes

The removal of political borders has also brought changes to the political landscape. Changes within states are evident in the hierarchy of government and its responsibility for the delivery of services and the election of public officials. In some places, order at the grass roots has broken down. The local state, which often receives few resources from the national state, may be bankrupt.

In parts of Eastern and Southeastern Europe, the federal state exerts little or no direct influence on decisions made by or affecting the lives of people locally. Instead, the new national mafias and clan warlords comprise the main political actors. Although these actors undermine the viability and credibility of the existing state, they may also be responsible for organizing citizen groups, providing effective opposition to the national government through the support of new political parties, and administering a variety of local public services including safety and police protection, transportation, schooling, water and sewage, and health care.

Some states in and near the border areas have had to find places for refugees. Some refugees are persons who were forced to move because of civil strife and ethnic cleansing, for example in the former Yugoslavia and the Caucasus. Others leave their home countries to seek a better life in the West. In some countries, abandoned military facilities serve as refugee camps.

Another change evident in the political landscape are the changed signs near the border and within the state itself. Older propaganda signs with heavy official ideological, party, police, and military overtones have been replaced by large and colorful welcome signs, often printed in several languages. Many towns, streets, parks, schools, cultural centers, and sports arenas have been renamed. Names commemorating now-discredited government leaders, outside military forces, and ideological references to unpopular events in recent history are removed. Many places (such as St. Petersburg in Russia) reverted to pre-Communist names; others are renamed for heroes and heroines of the recent transition period or to commemorate recent events. Statues and monuments commemorating Lenin, Stalin, and other historical figures of the Communist period have been torn down and destroyed, or carried off to the basements of nearby museums.

Openness is also marked by the emergence of new political parties. The names of these new parties signal the transition to democracy; hence words like *freedom, liberty, justice, unity*, and *people's* are often part of the new parties' names. Gone are words like *workers* and even *socialist* and *communist*. The membership of the new parties consists of old and new faces. Some leaders have adopted new party labels and campaign rhetoric while retaining their old views, whereas others are advocates of true political and economic reform.

Not unexpectedly, parties and voters facing the new political openness are addressing issues involving national identity. How important is ethnicity in one's identity? These questions may lead to the emergence of ethnic conflicts, not only within a state but also with other countries. In some areas, conflicts have involved language. Disputes center on the language of instruction in schools, in the new media, in government publications, and on street and road signs. Linguistic, religious, and cultural diversity may be identified with newly emerging political parties. Other conflicts involve the citizenship rights of members of ethnic groups. This is especially pronounced in states that have arisen following the breakup of larger multiethnic states such as the Soviet Union. In Estonia, conflict continues over the citizenship rights of persons of Russian ethnic ancestry, many of whom had been encouraged to move to Estonia by the Soviets.

The rights of women in border areas are changing. Women are now discovering the rights and privileges enjoyed by women in open countries across their borders. These issues include not only economic opportunities and their role as mothers and wives but also in their participation as equals in community, regional, and national politics and decision making. The rights of immigrants from once-closed states in Eastern Europe and the former Soviet Union is another ticklish issue. How governments deal with these human rights may affect entry of a state into an expanded European Union or the availability of loans or financial investment from Western Europe.

New Personal Landscapes

Many other changes are affecting the personal lives of individuals. These changes include new-found freedoms, exposure to new values, the creative forces of dynamic market economies, and fledgling democracies.

Changes such as these can be seen in various small but important ways on the landscape. Local residents take pride in newly painted houses, outside decorations such as shutters and gates, and attractive flower and vegetable gardens. Whereas a newly painted house once signaled special treatment or privileges granted to the resident by someone in power, now one can have a freshly painted house without raising suspicion or intimidation from neighbors. Pride in ownership encourages people to care for their properties. The plethora of small shops, businesses, and roadside stands represents private initiative.

Many persons now cross newly opened borders to work for higher wages in nearby, richer states. Daily commutes from Slovakia to Vienna and from western Slovenia to Trieste in northeastern Italy are popular. These individuals can purchase luggage, special household items, and other goods unavailable in good quality in their own countries. At the same time, residents of the more expensive country can traverse the border in the opposite direction in order to buy food, everyday clothing, and other staple items at lower costs.

In short, the open borders have brought about a series of changes to those on both sides of the once fenced borders. Families and friends once separated can now interact more easily. Persons can travel or work on the other side of the border without government restrictions. Open borders mean new freedoms for those long denied basic rights of mobility, visitation, purchase, investment and expression.

The Harsh Realities of Change

Without a doubt, openness has brought many welcome changes to the former East European countries. Yet openness has ushered in some unforeseen problems to those formerly closed states and to communities along international borders.

New-found freedoms and openness have brought wealth to some, but poverty to others, especially the sick, the elderly, the disabled, and those with large families. Prices for basic goods have skyrocketed while salaries have remained static. Unemployment has increased and many have had to travel long distances to search for work. Many families live at or below the poverty line, and higher rates of divorce and alcoholism have surfaced. Democracy and ethnic strife exist side by side. The threat of return to repressive political order threatens many of these fragile democratic states.

Freedoms are accompanied by a host of changes to the public and private sectors and to groups and individuals. Criminal activity has increased. In response, cars are locked and double-locked and houses have extra security locks. Business owners hire private security forces, not only to prevent individual criminal acts but also to thwart various gangs and mafias. Prostitution represents another growth service that is emerging as a result of the end of the Cold War. Drug traffic is also associated with selected ports and cities along major river and highway networks between eastern and central Europe. A medical problem that one seldom hears about in Eastern Europe is the increase in cases of Acquired Immune Deficiency Syndrome (AIDS). Socialist eastern Europe once denied the existence of many AIDS cases, but today it is suspected that rates of AIDS incidence have increased sharply with greater movement of human traffic across southern and eastern Europe.

Materialism and rampant consumerism have become evident in daily life, in newspaper and magazine stories and advertisements, movies and television as well as in the dress, lifestyles, language, and consumption habits of world-famous actors, rock stars, athletes, and other celebrities. Although many households cannot afford desired items, the American and Western European market economies are driving changes in social values. Eastern Europe is fast becoming a society where money means everything.

Openness and Teaching

How has education been affected by the open borders of Eastern Europe? Openness enables teachers to establish contacts with colleagues throughout the world. Teachers have e-mail accounts, send and receive faxes, and can apply for grants to study and visit abroad without securing government approval. Teachers can now receive many previously unavailable materials and resources. Books, magazines, journals, and cassettes come through the mail unopened. Many teachers are desperate to obtain access to these resources as they strive to prepare themselves and their students for the rapidly changing world. Teachers have found that they must use English to be able to function effectively in the post-Cold War world. Russian, the language of imperialism, is out while English is in. Classes in English are very popular in urban and rural areas throughout Eastern Europe.

At the same time, many teachers are struggling with the realities of day-to-day life in a rapidly changing society. Because prices have increased drastically without a corresponding increase in salaries, many teachers and other professionals find that they must hold additional part-time jobs in order to feed their families. Travel to professional meetings is often expensive, and teachers must spend their personal savings to attend. Skyrocketing costs have forced school officials to tighten their belts. Teachers are faced with insufficient quantities of basic supplies such as paper, chalk, and erasers. Textbooks and maps are outdated and incorrect. Librarians are forced to cancel subscriptions to newspapers, magazines, and journals because they are too expensive.

Conclusion

Changes in the world political map resulting from the end of the Cold War have affected the local geographies of communities in Eastern Europe dramatically. In examining these changes, we often focus our attention on dramatic changes that result from open borders—for example the exchanges of presidents and high government officials and conferences involving delegations of high-level officials in trade, finance, science, and culture. It is equally important to examine how these changes in the world political map have affected people in local communities. The daily lives of people and the communities in which they live, work, shop, interact, and worship have undergone profound change, as documented in this chapter. Teachers can do much to help in understanding the transitions associated with movement from isolation to cooperation, or from closed to open spaces.

References

Agnew, J. and S. Corbridge 1995. *Mastering Space: Hegemony, Territory, and International Political Economy.* London: Routledge.

Demko, G. J. and W. B. Wood eds. 1994. *Reordering the World: Geopolitical Perspectives on the Twenty-First Century.* Boulder, Colo.: Westview Press.

Johnston, R. J. and P. J. Taylor 1989. *A World in Crisis: Geopolitical Perspectives.* Oxford: Blackwell.

Kegley, C. W., Jr. and G. Raymond 1994. *A Multipolar Peace? Great Power Politics in the Twenty-First Century.* New York: St. Martin's Press.

Taylor, P. J. 1990. *Britain and the Cold War.* London: Pinter.

_____. 1994. "The State as Container: Territoriality in the Modern World System," *Progress in Human Geography*, 18: 151-162.

Part II: United States Perspectives

CHAPTER 6

GEOGRAPHIC IMPLICATIONS OF DEVOLUTION AND CHANGE IN THE AMERICAN FEDERAL SYSTEM

Janet E. Kodras

The American federal system is a distinctive form of government that shares its decision-making power among different levels (national, state, local) and different branches (executive, legislative, and judicial), with no single unit holding supreme authority. The Constitution and Bill of Rights specifically divide certain powers within the federal hierarchy. For example, the national government is responsible for regulating foreign commerce, issuing U.S. currency and declaring war. States are responsible for conducting elections and establishing local governments. The Constitution, however, does not specifically define many government powers and services. As a result, the search for appropriate divisions of responsibility between the national, state, and local governments is an ongoing process within the U.S. federal system.

The power of the federal government expanded in response to the Great Depression of the 1930s and again during the 1960s period of postwar economic growth. During the 1970s, efforts to decrease the strength of the Federal government relative to the states emerged. These efforts accelerated in the 1980s and took on new force in 1994 after a Republican majority in the House of Representatives introduced the *Contract with America.*

Although the national government is currently the stronger partner, the 50 states and more than 80,000 local governments exert substantial authority, and the distribution of benefits and burdens conferred by the government is still largely affected by the place in which one lives (see also Chapter 7). The amount of taxes one pays, the penalty for committing a crime, the control over land uses, the level of public school expenditures, the availability of public assistance, the extent of subsidies for housing, jobs, and economic development, and many other regulations and rules shaping the lives of Americans vary substantially from state to state and from place to place across the United States. Changing the structure of the federal system, as currently debated under the *Contract with America* and related proposals, geographically rearranges these benefits and burdens conferred by government and redistributes power and resources among places.

All American citizens need to understand the complex and ever-changing system of government that affects our individual lives and collective well-being. The National Geography Standards, which were established as one component of the *Goals 2000: Educate America Act* (Public Law 103-227), provide a blueprint for building this understanding. Specifically, Standard 13 in *Geography for Life: National Geography Standards* (1994: 91) sets precise targets for students at the K-12 levels to learn their position within the local-to-global divisions of political space and how these divisions affect their lives:

The interlocking systems for dividing and controlling Earth's space influence all dimensions of people's lives, including trade, culture, citizenship and voting, travel, and self-identity. Students must understand the genesis, structure, power, and pervasiveness of these divisions to appreciate their role within a world that is both globally interdependent and locally controlled.

The purpose of this chapter is to apply Standard 13 to the issue of the changing American federal system, and in particular, the current efforts to decrease the size and scope of the national government relative to states and localities. I focus on approaches to teaching political geography that may help students discover and understand the changing federal system and its role in American life. I begin with a general framework for studying the geographic structure and restructuring the American government that gives instructors an overall picture of the issue as a basis for developing classroom activities, and then draw upon this framework to describe specific learning activities that instructors can use to help their students creatively explore our ever-changing federal system in the United States. These are divided into activities for students at the elementary, junior high, and senior high school levels, according to guidelines set by Standard 13 for the fourth, eighth, and twelfth grades.

A Geographic Framework for Studying the Changing Federal System

The Geographers Network on Politics in America (GNPA) is a consortium of scholars who study geographic dimensions of the United States government and the variable effects of governmental restructuring on people living in different places across the country. The overall objectives are to facilitate public awareness of the great geographic complexities of governance in the United States and to help policy makers incorporate this perspective as an explicit part of their deliberations and policy choices. GNPA works from the supposition that an explicitly geographical perspective on governmental restructuring is of great value; that this perspective has not sufficiently been brought to bear in current debates; and that important decisions will be better informed to the extent that they recognize the geographic complexity of both the causes and the consequences of proposed governmental changes. GNPA has developed a general conceptual framework for the geographical analysis of governmental restructuring and has set a research agenda that uses this geographic perspective in the analysis of current proposals for governmental change (GNPA 1996). Following is a summary of this framework as a basis for instructors planning classroom activities on this topic.

The framework, shown in Figure 6.1, consists of three important elements: the *causes* of governmental change that are based in a geographically diverse American society (cell 1); the *types* of governmental change, such as devolution, privatization, and program dismantling (cell 2); and the place-specific *consequences* of governmental change (cell 3). A brief discussion of geographic aspects of the causes, types, and consequences of governmental change is followed by illustrations of how this framework can be used to study one of the most significant changes in American public policy, the Supreme Court decision on public school desegregation.

Figure 6.1 Linking the Causes, Types, and Consequences of Government Restructuring

CELL 1	**Changes in Society**
	changing local contexts of social, economic, political, and environmental conditions that *cause* changes in government
CELL 2	**Changes in Government**
	types of government restructuring, including devolution, privatization, dismantling of government programs and services
CELL 3	**Changes in Society**
	changing local contexts of social, economic, political, and environmental conditions that are the *consequence* of changes in government

Causes of Governmental Restructuring

The current upheavals in the United States government are related to complex changes occurring in American society. The dominance of the United States over international affairs has undergone significant change since the mid-1960s and the U.S. government has lost some of its leverage over the domestic economy, as global corporations and international agreements, such as NAFTA and GATT, exert increasing control. In addition, rising numbers of Americans face economic insecurity through increasing unemployment or underemployment, falling wages, declining benefits, and dwindling savings. These recent economic changes have reduced the ability of the federal government and the willingness of many taxpayers to support services previously performed by government. Economic decline and social fragmentation increasingly are expressed in political discontent and reconsideration of the legitimate role of government in a changing American society.

These societal changes are redrawing the map of the American economic and political systems.

For example, the decline of midwest manufacturing in the 1970s led to severe economic stagnation in cities throughout the region, accompanied by an explosion of urban social problems, a decline in the tax base of municipalities, and an intensification of racial segregation. In the 1980s, small towns and rural areas in the country's interior were hard hit as a result of crises in agriculture and resource extraction industries, especially petroleum. Meanwhile, the growth of manufacturing and services in the South and on the West Coast during the last two decades has generated interregional population migrations, and therefore political realignment, away from Democratic strongholds in the Northeast and North Central states toward the more conservative South and West. At the local scale, increasing residential segregation has deepened the division of electoral districts according to class, race, and national origin, resulting in the growing power of suburban districts, spatially and socially separated from the problems of inner cities or rural areas.

Congressional redistricting since 1990 has also played a role, spatially rearranging the margins of support for the two leading parties and thus bringing new members to the House of Representatives. In the 1994 election, redistricting, open-seat contests, and the place-specific expression of economic and social frustrations in districts across the country brought Republican majorities to both houses. This new power base has sought to capture the wellsprings of social and economic discontent by establishing its vision of the role of government within American society (Kodras *et al.* 1997).

Types of Governmental Restructuring

The defining document in the most recent effort to restructure government is the *Contract with America*, introduced on January 1995 by the new Republican majority in the 104th Congress. The contract and subsequent proposals advocate rapid reduction in the size and scope of the national government, devolving federal responsibilities to states and localities, shifting functions to the private sector and civic institutions, dismantling regulations, and in some cases eliminating programs and funding altogether.

Devolution is the decentralization of government responsibilities and resources from higher to lower levels of the federal hierarchy. Devolution often involves a reorganization of agencies and programs, a shift of authority across levels or administrative units of government, a change in the entitlement of citizens or corporations to government services or benefits, a shift in access to government services, or a redefinition of the government's responsibilities for regulating society. These internal transformations within the federal hierarchy often rearrange the geographic distribution of who pays and who receives government services.

Privatization, by contrast, shifts the provision of services from government to external, non-governmental organizations, with assets and responsibilities transferred to the private sector. Examples of government's encouragement of, and entanglements with, the private sector include the establishment of quasi-government corporations (such as the U.S. Postal Service), the use of private contractors (such as contracts made to firms that clean environmentally damaged areas), and the use of vouchers and subsidies to be spent in the private sector (such as food stamps).

Dismantling occurs when the government stops providing a service, withdraws regulations, or terminates funding of particular activities no longer deemed appropriate. In this case, the activities will either cease to exist or will fall to market or voluntary ventures for their maintenance. Whether governmental restructuring occurs through devolution, privatization, or dismantling, the geographic distribution of government resources and responsibilities is altered in the process.

The Consequences of Governmental Restructuring

The effects of government restructuring are largely a function of the place in which one lives. Even across-the-board changes adopted at the national level are implemented within the diverse economic, social, political, and environmental contexts of different places. When government restructuring involves devolution of responsibility to states and local governments or shifting responsibilities to a highly segmented private sector, local context becomes even more important in generating geographic variations in government provision.

To understand the concept of local context, consider that each local place in the United States has distinctive economic characteristics (e.g., based on local resource endowments and production systems), social relations (e.g., defined by class, race, ethnicity, gender, generation), and political conditions (e.g., based on party politics, local civic traditions, ideologies, nongovernmental institutions). These economic, social, and political characteristics combine to create the place-specific context in which government operates, and, indeed, the local sense of what is appropriate and possible for government to undertake.

Places, therefore, are not passive recipients of changes dictated by the national government. Rather, they are actively engaged in the politics of policy design and implementation. The needs and demands of the local population and firms affect the extent to which a proposed change at the federal level is even considered relevant and deserving of attention. The capacity of local institutions, both within and outside the formal government, determines whether sufficient resources, expertise, and infrastructure are available to address a political issue, and local power relations influence how they can address and resolve the issue. As a result, any change in the U.S. federal system has geographically variable consequences across the country, as each place interprets that change within its particular local context.

Applying the Framework: The Example of Public School Desegregation

The conceptual framework presented in Figure 6.1 illustrates how transformations in a geographically-diverse American society (cell 1) can generate demands to change the form and functions of government, itself spatially-structured and geographically-complex (cell 2), and the resultant restructuring has place-specific effects in the further transformation of society (cell 3).

The case of school desegregation brings this framework to life and demonstrates its real-world importance for understanding governmental change and its influences on the lives of Americans. By the 1950s, residential segregation by race and income level was a notable feature of American life. In the North, discriminatory practices in employment and housing tended to generate racially homogenous school districts, while in the South, Jim Crow laws officially separated blacks and whites into different schools. Most children as a result attended school with others of the same racial and class background and the quality of education provided in schools serving low-income black children was demonstrably inferior. The spatial structures of race and class in the United States generated notable inequities in the provision of education.

Policies and programs designed and implemented at the most decentralized level, by local school boards, resulted in spatial inequalities in education that required resolution at the most centralized government level, the U.S. Supreme Court. The Court's 1954 landmark decision in *Brown v. Board of Education of Topeka, Kansas* ruled that racial segregation in education was unconstitutional, and later rulings mandated busing students to equalize the racial composition of schools within districts.

This national policy had dramatic geographic consequences. First, its applicability varied regionally, according to the racial composition of local school districts. The effects of and resistance to the rulings were at first greatest in the South, where city-wide districts included both blacks and whites. In the North, where racially homogenous districts were the norm, *de facto* segregation persisted for some time. Second, the policy played a role in the geographic transformation of many urban areas since that time, as millions of white residents moved to largely affluent suburban areas. The presence of independent and predominantly white suburban school districts was an important factor in these changes. We continue to experience the effects of this migration today, with a host of social and financial problems facing cities—problems that now generate pressure for new governmental policy and programs. The question of how to respond to the social and economic conditions in today's urban areas figures prominently in current debates about the functions and role of government.

Using Standard 13 to Study the Changing Federal System

How can the framework be used to develop classroom activities? Standard 13 identifies specific targets for learning about political divisions of space and how government services and political power are allocated across the different levels of the American federal system (*Geography for Life: National Geography Standards* 1994: 130-131, 169-170, 210-211). These guidelines can help instructors to design classroom activities for students to explore how and why government services and political power are redistributed among levels of the federal system, and the implications of these shifts for people living in different places across the country.

Activities for Students in Elementary School

Standard 13 states that by the end of fourth grade, students should understand the types and basic characteristics of political units from the local to global levels, such as the school district, community, county, state, and country in which they live (*Geography for Life: National Geography Standards* 1994, 130-131). As applied to the concerns of this chapter, students in elementary school first need to learn the different types of government and where they live within these, as well as the basic types and characteristics of a few government programs or services (Figure 6.1, cell 2)

Finding Your Place in the World. Instructors can help students understand where they live within the many governments that affect them and their families with a game using a set of political maps. The instructor prepares for the game by obtaining maps at a variety of scales. Students gather around a table to study the maps, locating where they live and go to school on the community map, where their community is located on a county map, where their county is located on a state map, and on up to the global level. The instructor can help students learn about the important concept of scale by showing how each map is a small area on the next map from the local to the global scales. This will also improve students' appreciation of where they live on the Earth's globe.

Learning about the National School Lunch Program. Students in elementary school can also begin to learn about government programs. Teaching students about government programs is easiest if the program is something that directly affects them. Instructors can prepare for this lesson by reading about this and related programs. For example, the National School Lunch Program (NSLP) provides hot lunches to school children at reduced rates. The federal government provides food and cash assistance to participating public and private schools. The program uses three payment plans, with the price set for a child's lunch depending on the family's economic circumstances. Even children who pay full price benefit from the program because the government helps the school cover food costs and pay lunchroom workers. After the instructor teaches students some basic information about the National School Lunch Program, students can interview the school principal and head of the cafeteria to learn about how this program of the U.S. government works in their school. In 1995 Congress considered eliminating the National School Lunch Program, but as of this writing there are no concrete plans to dismantle the program. If Congress does alter or eliminate the NSLP, students can talk about how this change in a government program affects what they eat for lunch.

Activities for Students in Junior High School

Standard 13 states that by the end of eighth grade, students should understand the different government service areas and their functional relation to the student's own world (*Geography for Life: National Geography Standards* 1994: 169-170). As applied to the concerns of this chapter, students in junior high school can begin to sort out the different levels of government that provide government programs and services (Figure 6.1, cell 2), and to see that where they live affects the types of government services made available to them and their families (Figure 6.1, cell 3).

Learning about the Geographic Coverage of Government Programs. Students can best understand the complex geographic arrangements of government programs in the United States by creating and analyzing maps of important characteristics of those programs. The current debates in the U.S. Congress concern devolution of programs from the national to the state level in the federal hierarchy, so it is especially appropriate for our purposes to study maps of interstate variations in government programs. Instructors can obtain these maps, or the data needed for students to create their own maps, from a number of sources. The Geographers Network on Politics in America (GNPA) maintains a website that provides maps of interstate variations in participation, funding, and effects of government programs, and as well as maps of changes in these variables over time. A text accompanies each map series that summarizes the purpose and history of the program as well as an explanation of geographic variations portrayed on the maps. Instructors can download and print these maps to provide information on the geographic distribution of government services.

For example, students might analyze how the states differ in per pupil expenditures in public schools. This map shows the amount expended per pupil, given average daily attendance in each state, so it controls for the different number of students living in different states. School expenditures are divided into three equal categories: the top one-third of states in terms of school funding, the middle third, and the bottom third. Instructors can help students gain an appreciation for the geography of government services by showing maps such as this one, and then asking which states show the highest values on this variable. Which show the lowest? Do states in the same category of this variable cluster together to form regions of high or low government spending on public schools? What does this mean? What level of government spending is shown for your state? Why might it be higher or lower than its neighbors? Questions such as these will help students to interpret the geographic patterns of government programs.

Activities for Students in Senior High School

Standard 13 states that by the end of twelfth grade, students should understand the effect of different political arrangements on people's daily lives and how different political viewpoints play a role in conflicts over resources and territories (Geography for Life: National Geography Standards 1994: 210-211). As applied to the concerns of this chapter, students in senior high school should be able to comprehend the consequences of providing specific government services at different levels of the federal hierarchy. They should also be able to understand the implications of governmental restructuring and how these tie into larger political debates within American society. Specifically, students in senior high school can begin to explore all three elements of the conceptual framework identified in Figure 6.1.

Causes of Government Restructuring. First, students can question how changes in American society play out in different local contexts, generating place-specific demands for governmental restructuring (Figure 6.1, cell 1). Questions for classroom debate or group paper projects include:
  · How has recent economic growth or decline in your community/state/region affected politics in those places?
  · How did Congressional redistricting after 1990 alter the representation of different political parties and social movements in the House of Representatives?
  · How do people's direct experiences with government influence their attitudes about the appropriate level of government service provision and regulation?

Types of Government Restructuring. Second, students can learn about the different types of change in the American government, by studying which kinds of public policies are affected by devolution, privatization, or dismantling and how the geographic distribution of authority, resources, public employment, and funding is consequently rearranged (Figure 6.1, cell 2). Questions for study reports and classroom discussion include:
  · What are the advantages and disadvantages of returning power to the states during the cur-

rent period of federal devolution?

- When the national government sends money to the states, it adds certain rules and constraints on the way states can use that money. Why does the national government attach these conditions? Is this a threat to the principles of federalism?
- Why does the national government want to devolve certain responsibilities to lower levels of the federal hierarchy while keeping other functions to itself? Who decides?
- What kinds of government functions are best provided at the national level? At the state level? At the local level?
- Why would the government want to shift some of its responsibilities to the private sector? How does the government ensure that the private sector performs services in accordance with the needs and demands of citizens? Should the government maintain some control or oversight of services shifted to the private sector?
- How does your state and local government find the financial resources to take on responsibilities devolved by the national government?
- What charitable and other voluntary organizations exist in your area? Do these organizations have the resources needed to take on responsibilities shifted from government during privatization?

Consequences of Government Restructuring. Third, students can study the consequences of governmental change for different populations and places, examining how policy changes are implemented in specific places (Figure 6.1, cell 3). Specific questions for study and include:

- How do devolution and privatization affect access to health care and education in your community? Why might the effect vary in different places across the country?
- How do social program changes affect levels of poverty and hunger in your community? Why might these effects vary in different places across the country?
- Does the government have a responsibility to care for poor, sick, or disabled people in American society? What level of government is best suited to provide these programs? Give both the advantages and disadvantages of national versus state control of public welfare programs.
- How do budget and regulatory changes in environmental programs affect the quality of life in your community? Why might these effects vary in different places across the country?
- How can devolution of governmental responsibility to local communities open new opportunities for political participation and decision making? Are there any constraints on these opportunities?
- What influences the charitable generosity of individuals and organizations? How are these affected by charitable traditions in different places?
- How will devolution of government functions alter local political relationships, including the ability of different groups to participate in political decision-making?

Various resources are available for instructors and students to use in addressing these questions. As mentioned above, GNPA's website contains a time series of maps depicting the types of governmental changes currently underway and their emerging consequences in different parts of the country. The website also contains a bibliography that instructors and students in senior high school can use to read about these issues. The best way for students to learn about the effect of government changes in their community is to interview local government officials who are in charge of making these changes. Elected officials are often happy to visit a classroom to talk about local government. Individual students might also interview people who receive a government service, such as Social Security, a college loan, or food stamps and report to the class what the program means in the life of particular people.

Concluding Observations

The 1994 Congressional elections are widely regarded as a watershed event in American political and social history. The election of a Republican majority in both houses, including a large number of activist conservatives, and the rallying of those forces in the first concerted attempt by Congress in more than a century to set the course for the nation that portends dramatic changes in the scale and scope of government.

The general framework outlined in this chapter provides a geographical approach to investigate the current political controversies about what government can and should do and what level in the federal hierarchy should oversee different functions. It presents a pragmatic view of government as both affected by, and affecting, the larger society of which it is a part. Society exerts pressure to influence and direct government actions, and these actions in turn change society. The current forces calling for change in the scale and scope of American government are the latest in an ongoing effort to bring the rules of governance into conformance with the perceived needs and demands of society. No easy answers emerge on how this is to be done or what the effects will be, but an important element of the current public debates should be an explicit recognition that the implications of government restructuring will differ dramatically from place to place across the country, reflecting geographic variations in the resources and capacities of public and private institutions to address these changes, and given the great geographic diversity of the American people whose lives will be altered by the outcome. Instructors play a critical role in helping tomorrow's citizens understand the geographic complexities of an ever-changing American government.

References Cited

Geography for Life: National Geography Standards 1994. Washington, D.C.: National Geographic Research and Exploration for the American Geographical Society, Association of American Geographers, National Council for Geographic Education, and the National Geographic Society.

Geographers Network on Politics in America, 1996. *Geographic Perspectives on Governmental Restructuring: A Conceptual Framework and Research Agenda.* Working Paper #1. Woodrow Wilson School of Public Policy. Princeton, N. J : Princeton University.

Kodras, Janet E., Lynn R. Staeheli, and Colin Flint, editors 1997. *State Devolution in America.* Thousand Oaks, California: Sage.

Additional References for Instructors Wanting to Read Further

DiIulio, John J. Jr. and Donald F. Kettl. 1995. *Fine Print: The Contract with America, Devolution, and the Administrative Realities of American Federalism.* Report #CPM 95-1. Center for Public Management. Washington, D.C.: Brookings Institution.

Karger, Howard J. and David Stoesz 1994. *American Social Welfare Policy: A Pluralist Approach.* New York: Longman.

Kettl, Donald F. and John J. DiIulio, Jr. 1995. *Cutting Government.* Report #CPM 95-2, Center for Public Management. Washington, D.C.: Brookings Institution.

Kodras, Janet E. and John Paul Jones, III, editors. 1990. *Geographic Dimensions of Social Policy in the United States.* London: Edward Arnold.

Pagano, Michael A. and Ann O'M. Bowman 1995. "The State of American Federalism, 1994-1995." *Publius: The Journal of Federalism* 25,3: 1-21.

Peterson, Paul E. 1995. *The Price of Federalism.* Washington, D.C.: Brookings Institution.

U.S. Bureau of the Census. Decennial. *County and City Data Book.* Washington, D.C.: U.S. Government Printing Office.

U.S. Bureau of the Census. Annual. *Statistical Abstract of the United States.* Washington, D.C.: U.S. Government Printing Office.

CHAPTER 7
POLITICAL SPACE AND THE UNITED STATES
Gerald R. Webster

Geography National Standard 13 states (*Geography for Life* 1994: 91):

> The interlocking systems for dividing and controlling Earth's space influence all dimensions of people's lives, including trade, culture, citizenship and voting, travel, and self-identity. Students must understand the genesis, structure, power, and pervasiveness of these divisions to appreciate their role within a world that is both globally interdependent and locally controlled.

How should teachers approach the fulfillment of this Standard? What should they emphasize? Most certainly a discussion of the nearly 200 countries in the world today is important. An appreciation by American students of the earth's pattern of states and state power is unquestionably beneficial as our political, economic, and social systems become ever more globally interconnected (Johnson, Taylor, and Watts 1995). Equally important is understanding and appreciating the enormous influences on peoples' daily lives of the internal organization of political space within countries. Just as citizenship in any of the world's countries has enormous influences on an individual's life possibilities, as does one's residence in any of the 50 states, and their more than 80,000 general and special purpose local governments (Bullard, Grigsby, and Lee 1994).

Purpose

The United States is divided and subdivided into tens of thousands of units of political space that daily affect individuals. In addition, hundreds of other units of political space around the world daily influence the lives of U.S. citizens. Responsible citizenship requires students to understand the geographic and functional complexity of the system of jurisdictional subdivisions they will inherit and influence as adults. This chapter has two principal goals. First, it outlines its subject: the present geographic divisions of political space that powerfully affect the citizenry of the United States. The number of political subdivisions in the world and in the United States is growing. This chapter will argue that the processes leading to ever greater numbers of political subdivisions in the United States and around the world are fundamentally the same.

Political Functions

What are the basic functions that subdivisions of political space fulfill? Soja (1971: 7) identifies three principal categories of political functions. These are the 1) control function over the distribution, allocation, and ownership of scarce resources, 2) the maintenance of order and the enforcement of authority, and 3) the creation and maintenance of institutions and behavior patterns that promote group unity and cohesiveness. From Soja's perspective government functions in political spaces to coordinate competition, limit conflict, and encourage cooperation—all of particularly critical importance in a capitalist democracy (see also Johnston 1982, chapter 2). Adopting this generalized perspective, an evaluation of units of political space might question whether the existing structure facilitates or thwarts the fulfillment of these functions.

Model of Governmental Tiers

Figure 7.1 provides examples of the governmental and quasi-governmental levels that might be identified as affecting U.S. citizens. At the top of the hierarchy is the best known example of a *Worldwide* political-governmental organization, the United Nations (Commission on Global Governance 1995). Below the *Worldwide* level in Figure 7.1's hierarchy are several *World Regional* organizations, most of which can be classified as "supranational" or "non-governmental organizations" (NGOs) that can exert substantial political influences, if not directly political purposes (Cooke 1993; Drake 1994). The growth in NGOs alone has been dramatic: in 1909 there were but 176 NGOs involving three or more countries, whereas today they number nearly 29,000 (Commission on Global Governance 1995: 32). Among the better known *World Regional* organizations are the Organization of African Unity (OAU), Arab League, Organization of American States (OAS), and the European Union (EU).

The basic political subdivision of the earth's surface is the *state*, approximately 200 of which exist today (Fig. 7.1). Though not all countries in the world are members of the United Nations (e.g., Switzerland), its membership rolls further underscore the growth in the size and complexity of the international community. At its creation in 1945, there were 51 members. By 1960 membership had doubled to 100, by 1980 it had tripled to 154, and today it stands at 185 countries (Plischke 1978; Committee on Global Governance 1995: 8). Given what Johnson (1995; see also Keyfitz 1995) calls the "Renaissance of Nationalism," it is possible that changes in the boundaries of countries in Eastern Europe and the area of the Russian Federation, among others, will cause the membership of the UN to top 200 by the year 2000—a quadrupling of member states in little more than a half century.

Sub-National Geographic Units

From the perspective of the preceding discussion, the U.S. central or federal government is one of nearly 200 players, albeit of disproportionate significance, in the international community of states. Although its authority within the boundaries of the geographic area of the United States is preeminent, it shares the responsibilities of governance with more than 80,000 other governmental entities, most significant of which are the 50 *First Order Civil Divisions* or state governments that are constitutional partners in the American system of federalism (Fig. 7.1).

Those drafting the Constitution certainly recognized that different governmental functions are best provided at different geographic scales. They delegated the "conduct of war" to the federal government, but left the control of local governments and education to the states. What necessary governmental functions, should be addressed at a regional or *Interstate Scale* that either the area of a single state or the federal government cannot adequately provide?

The best examples of such *Interstate Scale* geographic units are the more than 120 currently interstate compacts in effect (Fig. 7.1) (Welch and Clark 1973; Nice 1987). Analogous to treaties between countries, and involving substantially contrasting numbers of signatories, the average state in the United States is a party to more than twenty such cooperative agreements. Varied in purpose, interstate compacts now address joint concerns in education, environmental protection, law enforcement, social programs, and business and commercial activities.

Intra-State General Purpose Geographic Units

As noted earlier, the U.S. Constitution left the organization of local government to the states. Great variability exists between the types, functions, and numbers of local governments across the United States. Secondly, local governments have no authority independent of the states themselves, and their powers are typically defined in the constitutions of the respective states.

The *Second-Order Political Subdivision* in the United States is the county, 3,043 of which existed in 1992 (Fig. 7.1, Table 1). (In Louisiana *parishes* fulfill county functions, and in Alaska *borough* governments constitute the county equivalent.) Although county units exist in all states, counties in Connecticut and Rhode Island have no organized governments. In other circumstances county governments have consolidated or merged with municipalities, and are classified as municipal governments (Lyons 1977; Webster 1984).

General Purpose, Special Purpose, and Quasi-Governmental Units:
Inter-Tier Geographic and Functional Overlap

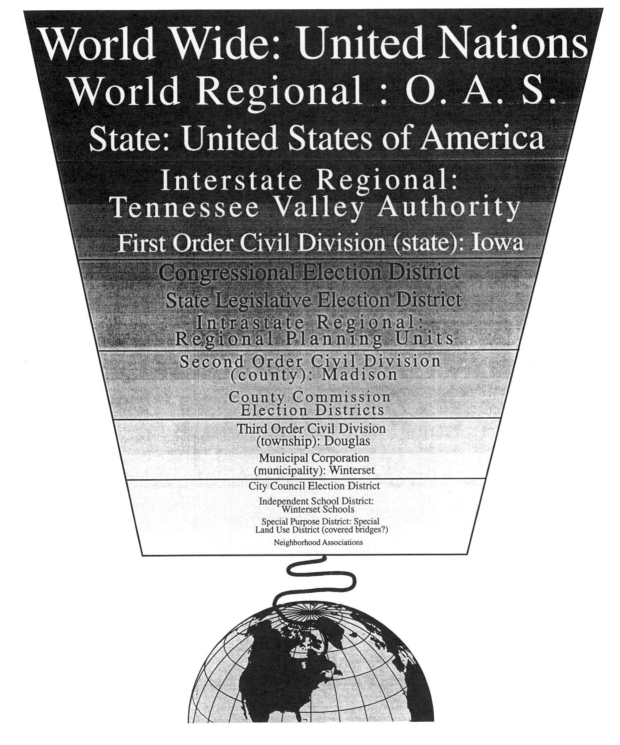

Figure 7.1   General Purpose, Special Purpose, and Quasi-Governmental Units:
Inter-Tier Geographic and Functional Overlap

Table 7.1. Local Government Types and Numbers in the U.S., 1952-1992

Type	1952	1962	1972	1982	1987	1992	Change 1952-1992	Change 1982-1992
GENERAL PURPOSE								
Counties or Equivalents	3,052	3,043	3,044	3,041	3,042	3,043	-9 -0.3%	+2 +0.0
Municipalities	16,807	17,997	18,517	19,076	19,200	19,296	+2,489 +14.8%	+220 +1.1%
Townships	17,202	17,144	16,991	16,734	16,691	16,666	-536 -3.2%	-68 -0.4%
SPECIAL PURPOSE								
School Districts	67,355	34,678	15,781	14,851	14,721	14,556	-52,799 -78.4%	-295 -2.0%
Special Districts	12,340	18,323	23,885	28,078	29,532	33,131	+20,791 +168.5%	+5,053 +18.0%
Total	**116,756**	**91,185**	**78,218**	**81,780**	**83,186**	**86,692**	**-30,064 -25.7%**	**+4,912 +6.0%**
Population*	151,684	180,671	205,052	227,757	248,710	255,078	+103,394 +68.0%	+27,321 +12.0%
P/P/L/G**	1,299	1,981	2,621	3,335	2,990	2,868	+1,569 +120.8%	-467 -14.0%

*In 1000s; all totals are for nearest census year or recent estimate

**Persons Per Local Government.

Source: U. S. Department of Commerce, Bureau of the Census, Census of Governments, *Governmental Organization*, 1992.

The *Third-Order Political Subdivision* in the United States is the township or town, 16,666 of which existed in 1992 (Fig. 7.1, Table 7.1) (U.S. Department of Commerce 1992). Although these general purpose sub-county governments exist in twenty Northeastern and Midwestern states, only the state of Indiana's area is entirely subdivided into townships. Typical Midwestern townships are 36 square miles in area, their square shapes corresponding to the range and tier land survey system. Though appropriate for the needs of an agrarian society, functioning township governments have become fewer in number with improved transportation systems and as the country has become increasingly urbanized. Between 1952 and 1992 the number of townships dropped from 17,202 to 16,660, a decline of 536 or three percent.

Municipalities (municipal corporations) constitute another category of general purpose governments (Fig. 7.1). In 1992, 154 million Americans, 62 percent of all residents, lived in areas with municipal governments (Table 7.1) (U.S. Department of Commerce 1992: 12). Secondly, and unlike the slow but steady decline in townships, the number of municipalities continues to experience steady growth. In 1952 there were 16,807 incorporated municipalities, the number in 1992 was 19,297, an increase of nearly 2,500 during the past four decades. Also notable is that slightly more than half of all municipalities in 1992 had less than 1,000 inhabitants (U.S. Department of Commerce 1992, VI).

Special Intra-State Geographic Units

In addition to the thousands of general purpose governments such as states, counties, townships and municipalities, are more than fourteen thousand *school districts* and more than thirty-three thousand *special districts* in the United States (Fig. 7.1). Together these two categories of local government account for more than half the number of total governmental units enumerated by the

1992 Census of Governments.

In 1952 the United States contained more than 67,355 independent school districts; by 1992 their number had decreased by nearly 79 percent to 14,556 (Table 7.1). (Another 1,400 public school systems are technically agents of other governments, whether states, counties, townships, or municipalities.) Most of the decline in the numbers of independent public school systems can be attributed to consolidation of single-school districts in rural areas with few students (Honey 1983: 237-241; Shelley 1994). Improved road and transportation systems now allow students to be transported via bus to a single school that serves an area previously subdivided by several schools, or school districts.

In terms of numbers, the fastest growing type of governmental unit in the United States are special districts (Table 7.1). In 1952 there were 12,340 special districts—in 1992 their number was 33,131, a 168 percent increase. Between 1982 and 1992 alone the number of special districts increased by 5,053, or 18.0 percent. Nine states (California, Colorado, Illinois, Kansas, Missouri, Nebraska, Pennsylvania, Texas and Washington) each have more than 1,000 special districts. Four states (California, Illinois, Pennsylvania and Texas) have more than 2,000 with the state of Illinois having the largest number of special districts at 2,920 in 1992.

What are special districts? The Census Bureau defines special districts as "independent, special purpose governmental units that exist as separate entities with substantial administrative and fiscal independence from general purpose governments" (U.S. Department of Commerce 1992, VII). The overwhelming majority of special districts are single-function, having responsibilities for natural resources (20 percent), fire protection (16 percent), housing and community development (11 percent), water supply (10 percent), sewerage (6 percent), cemeteries (5 percent), parks (4 percent), libraries (3 percent), hospitals (2 percent), or airports (1 percent) (Table 7.2).

Table 7.2 Special District Local Governments by Function

Function	Number	Percent
Single Function Districts		
Natural Resource	6,564	19.8
Fire Protection	5,354	16.2
Housing and Community Development	3,663	11.1
Water Supply	3,442	10.4
Sewerage	1,850	5.6
Cemeteries	1,646	5.0
Parks and Recreation	1,212	3.7
Libraries	1,063	3.2
Education[a]	870	2.6
Hospitals	774	2.3
Highways	666	2.0
Health	619	1.9
Utilities[b]	479	1.4
Airports	447	1.3
Other	1,808	5.5
Multiple Function Districts	2,674	8.1
Total	**33,131**	**100.0**

[a] Primarily school building authorities.

[b] Other than water supply. Includes electric power, gas supply, and public transit.

Source: U.S. Department of Commerce, Bureau of the Census, (1992), *Census of Governments: Government Organization*, Washington, D.C.: U.S. Government Printing Office.

Why are the numbers of special districts growing so rapidly? The potential answers to this question are both numerous and complex (see Glassner 1996, chapter 14). Part of the answer lies in the geographic scales of existing governmental units that frequently are too small (or too large) for the effective provision of a given public good or service. A particular watershed may exceed the area of a single county, and to maintain water quality in the entire watershed, a political subdivision exceeding the county in size may be created. In other cases an existing subdivision may simply lack the financial resources to support a valued or necessary function (e.g., library, landfill) and therefore join with surrounding areas to form a special district—nearly half of all special districts have independent taxing power (U.S. Department of Commerce 1992: 3).

In other cases the creation of new special districts may be a means of circumventing functional or fiscal restrictions upon the existing general purpose jurisdictions. For instance, if an existing local government has strict limits on how much debt it can assume, it might look upon the creation of a new special district positively if the new jurisdiction has additional debt authority. The creation of a special district may also be a response by a local population to improve the service for a specific function it believes is inadequately provided by the existing general purpose government. At present, this last justification is particularly common in growing (and subdividing) suburban areas in the United States (Danielson 1976; Zeigler and Brunn 1980; Foster 1993).

Inter-Local Geographical Units

As pointed out above, local areas are frequently subdivided by dozens of governmental jurisdictions. The average county in the United States contained more than 27 other local governments in 1992, although this number varied greatly (U.S. Department of Commerce 1992: 2). The counties of nine states averaged more than 50 local governments (California, Connecticut, Illinois, Massachusetts, New Hampshire, New Jersey, New York, North Dakota, and Pennsylvania), with California, Connecticut, New Jersey, and Pennsylvania having more than 70 local governments per county. This level of local government fragmentation can make area-wide planning and the provision of some area-wide services difficult. To aid in overcoming the problems associated with fragmentation, local governments may create *inter-local* units such as Councils of Government (COGs), scores of which exist across the country. Among other examples are regional planning districts or regions, now found in most states, that provide planning or other functions for groups of counties (Fig. 7.1).

Electoral Districts

The United States Constitution apportions representation in the House of Representatives to the states based on population. This subsequently led to the subdivision of states into districts for the purposes of electing members of the House, which today has 435 members (Morrill 1981; Webster 1995) (Fig. 7.1). Although congressional districts are not governmental units in the strict sense, they are central to our system of territorial representation (Archer and Shelley 1986, Chapter 1). Given that we elect our U.S. Senators statewide, states might be considered electoral districts as well. Most Americans also cast ballots for state senators and state representatives from districts, and counties and cities are generally subdivided into districts for the selection of members to the county commission, city council, planning commission, and school board, among many others.

Fragmentation of Political Space

As noted above, space is subdivided into political units to fulfill political functions. Central to the evaluation of political-geographic structures is whether they facilitate or thwart the fulfillment of these political functions. Does the structure of political space described above aid or defy the operation of government? As discussed below, the answer to this question is largely in the eye of the beholder.

International Fragmentation In recent years geographers and other scholars (e.g., Demko and

Wood 1994; Hooson 1994; Johnston, Taylor, and Watts 1995) gave the subject of nationalism considerable attention. This attention resulted in part from the growing globalization of the world economy, and the concomitant interdependence in the economic, social, and political relationships between the world's States. Keyfitz (1995: 208) has recently provided insight on why the community of States is now growing.

> Two ideals have dominated world politics for two hundred years. In one...called liberal, there are no real differences among peoples, and that they speak different languages and have different religions should not be allowed to affect their collaboration in a national state; the United States with its multiethnic, multinational composition has been the concrete expression of this. The opposite ideal, here called nationalist or reactionary, was that people ought to be able to live in a political community whose boundaries reflect that; Iran is an extreme case of this...the forces of separation seem on the rise, those of [a] union of multiculture nations, on the decline.

Keyfitz traces the liberal ideal back to the eighteenth century Enlightenment suggesting the Constitution of the United States reflects its view in such statements as "All men (sic) are created equal." We might label this view as "fusion." He traces the nationalist ideal to nineteenth century Romanticism arguing that the Romantics believed that "all people are decidedly not equal, and ethnic differences are by no means incidental—they are basic." Flowing from this vision, communities that "have lived side-by-side in peace for generations are suddenly torn apart; the land must be split so that each can have its own nation-state" (1995: 208-209). We might label this view as "fission," and look to recent events in Africa, the area of the former Soviet Union, and the Balkans for examples of its consequences (see Johnson 1995).

What might these two diametrically opposed views suggest about the size of the community of states? If we consider the Romantic view, the number of states in the world is far fewer than is appropriate, with the number of states being determined by the number of self-defined nations. On the African continent alone hundreds of language and tribal entities exist without the benefit of their own nation-state. Taken to the extreme the community of states could be several times larger than it is now.

From the vantage of the Enlightenment perspective, the current number of states is likely too large. Under their conception of humanity, material progress is of substantial importance, and market economics is "the only possible regulator of human relations (Keyfitz 1995: 209)." Taken to its farthest extreme, this view might well result in larger and larger territorial associations in an effort to maintain stability for international market processes. Economic markets benefit from the smooth flow of scarce resources, the maintenance of order, and populations pulling in the same direction. Arguably, the development of the European Union, potential extension of the NAFTA further into the Americas, or the case put forth by the UN's Committee on Global Governance (1995) for worldwide coordination, provide examples of the impulses stemming from this conception of the role of government.

Local Government Fragmentation The preceding discussion suggests the number of states on the earth's surface is in part the outgrowth of the opposing forces of fusion and fission, at present the latter seemingly gaining an upper hand. Is there an analogy between the growing number of world states resulting from a surge of nationalism, and the growth of jurisdictional fragmentation within the United States? Arguably both situations are the result of a growing acceptance of what Keyfitz (1995) refers to as the nationalist or reactionary belief that "all people are decidedly not equal," that differences between people are not "incidental" but "basic." Nationality and ethnicity are surely the dominant dimensions at the international level employed to justify the creation of new countries. If we add to nationality and ethnicity characteristics such as race, occupation, economic status, age, and lifestyle, the processes and results are quite similar.

This should be some cause for concern because of the implications for spatial equity between groups and places, and the potential endless fracturing of the landscape into smaller and smaller units. As noted in one popular geography textbook, "such balkanization...threatens the survival of some important democratic values that have prevailed throughout the evolution of U.S. society" (de Blij and Muller 1992: 205). Most important among these is Keyfitz's (1995: 208) liberal notion that differences between people in a country "should not be allowed to affect their collaboration in a national state." As he argued, "the United States with its multiethnic, multinational composition has been the concrete expression of this." This growing change in perspective might be viewed as a frontal assault on the assumptions of American democracy and pluralism.

Conclusions

This chapter serves a two-fold purpose. First, it briefly reviewed the multitude of units in political space that affect the citizenry of the United States. It then reviewed the circumstances of the growing number of world countries, followed by a discussion of the increasing fragmentation of governmental structures in the United States. It attempted to tie these two processes together, suggesting that they are similar in origin and result. In short, it argued these processes, though at fundamentally contrasting geographic scales were the result of growing rejection of the Enlightenment thesis that dissimilar people can successfully operate in the same political unit—a cornerstone of the United States' democratic system.

References Cited

Archer, J. Clark, and Fred M. Shelley 1986. *American Electoral Mosaics*. Washington, D.C.: Association of American Geographers.

Bullard, Robert D., J. Eugene Grigsby III, and Charles Lee, eds. 1994. *Residential Apartheid*. Los Angeles: CAAS Publications.

Commission on Global Governance. 1995. *Our Global Neighborhood*. New York: Oxford University Press.

Cooke, Philip. 1993, "Globalization of Economic Organisation and the Emergence of Regional Interstate Partnerships." Pp. 46-58 in *The Political Geography of the New World Order*, Colin H. Williams ed. London: Belhaven.

Danielson, Michael N. 1976. *The Politics of Exclusion*. New York: Columbia University Press.

de Blij, H. J., and Peter O. Muller 1992. *Geography: Regions and Concepts*, revised 6th ed., New York: John Wiley.

Demko, George J., and William B. Wood, eds. 1994. *Reordering the World*. Boulder: Westview.

Drake, Christine. 1994. "The United Nations and NGOs: Future Roles." Pp. 243-268 in *Reordering the World*, George Demko and William B. Wood eds. Boulder: Westview.

Foster, Kathryn A. 1993. "Exploring the Links Between Political Structure and Metropolitan Growth," *Political Geography*, 12(6): 523-547.

Geography for Life: National Geography Standards 1994. Washington, D.C.: National Geographic Research and Exploration for the American Geographical Society, Association of American Geographers, National Council for Geographic Education, and the National Geographic Society.

Glassner, Martin Ira 1996. *Political Geography, 2d ed. New York: John Wiley.*

Honey, Rex D. 1983. "Versatility versus Continuity—The Dilemma of Jurisdictional Change." Pp. 228-244 in *Pluralism and Political Geography*, Nurit Kliot and Stanley Waterman eds. New York: St. Martin's.

Hooson, David, ed. 1994. *Geography and National Identity.* Oxford: Blackwell.

Johnson, Nuala C. 1995. "The Renaissance of Nationalism." Pp. 97-110 in *Geographies of Global Change*, R. J. Johnston, Peter J. Taylor, and Michael J. Watts, eds. Oxford: Blackwell.

Johnston, R. J. 1982. *Geography and the State.* New York: John Wiley.

_____. 1990. "Local State, Local Government, and Local Administration." Pp. 59-73 in *The State in Action*, James Simmie and Roger King eds. London: Pinter Publishers.

_____, Peter J. Taylor, and Michael J. Watts 1995. *Geographies of Global Change.* Oxford: Blackwell.

Keyfitz, Nathan 1995. "Subdividing National Territories," *Geographical Analysis.* 27(3): 208-229.

Lyons, W. E. 1977. *The Politics of City-County Merger.* Lexington: University of Kentucky Press.

Morrill, Richard L. 1981. *Political Redistricting and Geographic Theory.* Washington, D.C.: Association of American Geographers.

Nice, David C. 1987. "State Participation in Interstate Compacts," *Publius*, 17(spring): 69-83.

Plischke, Elmer. 1978. "Microstates: Lilliputs in World Affairs," *Futurist*, February: 19-25.

Shelley, Fred M. 1994. "Local Control and Financing of Education: A Perspective from the American State Judiciary," *Political Geography*, 13(4): 361-376.

Soja, Edward W. 1971. *The Political Organization of Space.* Washington, D.C.: Association of American Geographers.

United States Department of Commerce, Bureau of the Census 1992. *Census of Governments: Government Organization.* Washington, D.C.: U.S. Government Printing Office.

Webster, Gerald R. 1984. "The Spatial Reorganization of County Boundaries in Kentucky," *Southeastern Geography*, 24(1): 14-29.

_____. 1995 "Congressional Redistricting in the Southeastern U.S. in the 1990s," *Southeastern Geographer*, 35(1): 1-21.

Welch, Susan, and Cal Clark 1973. "Interstate Compacts and National Integration: An Empirical Assessment of Some Trends," *Western Political Quarterly*, 26: 475-484.

Zeigler, Donald J., and Stanley D. Brunn 1980. "Geopolitical Fragmentation and the Pattern of Growth and Need: Defining the Cleavage between Sunbelt and Frostbelt Metropolises." Pp. 77-92 in *The American Metropolitan System: Present and Future*, Stanley D. Brunn and James O. Wheeler, eds. London: V. H. Winston and Sons.

CHAPTER 8
POLITICAL GEOGRAPHY AND VOTING RIGHTS IN THE UNITED STATES
Jonathan I. Leib

The year 1995 marked the 125th anniversary of the ratification of the Fifteenth Amendment to the U.S. Constitution. The Amendment states that the "right of citizens of the United States to vote shall not be denied or abridged by the United States or by any State on account of race, color, or previous condition of servitude." Over much of the following century, however, the Fifteenth Amendment was rarely enforced in the South. One of the key legislative accomplishments of the civil rights movement of the 1950s and 1960s, therefore, was the enactment of the Voting Rights Act of 1965, which allowed Federal intervention to ensure the rights of African Americans to vote.

The year 1995 was also one of controversy involving future interpretations of the Voting Rights Act. In June, the Supreme Court ruled Georgia's African-American population majority 11th Congressional District unconstitutional in *Miller v. Johnson*. The Court's decision called into question future applications of the Voting Rights Act because the district had been drawn at the insistence of the U.S. Department of Justice, which is charged with enforcing the Act.

In this chapter, we review the political geography of voting rights in the United States. The first part examines restrictions placed on minority voting rights from the late nineteenth to the mid-twentieth centuries. A discussion of the 1965 Voting Rights Act and the issue of minority vote dilution follows. The last part of this chapter provides an overview of recent court decisions that call into question attempts to increase the number of minority group members elected to public office in the 1990s. It concludes with a discussion of cumulative voting, which is an alternative to single-member district electoral systems that advocates claim is a better method for providing fair and effective representation.

This chapter illustrates an essential facet of National Geography Standard 13 (*Geography for Life* 1994: 90-91, 130-131, 169-170, 210-211). Historically, most political geography research has focused on the competition to divide and control vast areas of the earth's surface, such as countries and continents, and the resulting cooperation and conflict between groups over time. The debates over voting rights, however, demonstrate that the delimitation of and control over areas of the earth's surface as small as a city council or local school board district have also resulted in productive cooperation and destructive conflict between groups over time. Issues of voting rights and minority vote dilution are important issues to address in the classroom, because they directly affect students' abilities to influence the political system as they reach voting age (see Chapter 16).

Nineteenth and Twentieth Century Restrictions on Voting Rights

For twenty years after ratification of the Fifteenth Amendment, large numbers of newly enfranchised African Americans in the South voted in Presidential elections. Ninety-six percent of South Carolina's eligible African-American electorate voted in 1876, and more than ninety percent voted in 1880 elections in Tennessee and North Carolina (Kousser 1974). High rates of political participation translated into large numbers of African Americans being elected to office (Kousser 1992).

These rates began to drop in the 1890s because of white efforts that had the effect of eliminating the newly-won right to vote for virtually all southern African Americans (Kousser 1974; 1992). By 1940 only three percent of all voting age African Americans in the South were registered to vote, with less than one percent registered in the Deep South states of Alabama, Louisiana, Mississippi, and South Carolina (Garrow 1978). The combination of black disenfranchisement, the elimination of many poor whites from the political process, and the domination of the Democratic Party over the South meant that by the early twentieth century few southerners went to the polls (see Key 1949; Agnew 1987; Shelley et al. 1996). In presidential elections between 1904 and 1948, an average of only 26 percent of southerners eligible to vote according to the U.S. Constitution actually voted in each election (compared to 67 percent outside the South).

The Voting Rights Act of 1965

African-American registration rates began to increase slightly after World War II, although efforts to increase African-American voter registration met with intimidation and resistance. Resistance to black voter registration attempts were especially strong in Selma, a small rural city located in Dallas County in central Alabama. Although African Americans made up half of the county's population, by 1961 only 1 percent of voting-age African Americans in the county were registered to vote (Garrow 1978). With this background, Martin Luther King, Jr. decided to focus his efforts at ensuring voting rights in Selma. As King wrote in 1965 from his jail cell in Selma after being arrested during this effort:

> Why are we in jail? Have you ever been required to answer 100 questions on government, some abstruse even to a political science specialist, merely to vote? Have you ever stood in line with over a hundred others and after waiting an entire day seen less than ten given the [voter] qualifying test? This is Selma, Alabama, where there are more Negroes in jail with me than there are on the voting rolls (quoted in Williams 1987: 264).

The brutality waged against those protesting at Selma and elsewhere for voting rights shocked the country. In response, Congress passed the Voting Rights Act, which President Lyndon Johnson signed into law in August, 1965. The Act was enacted to guarantee and enforce the right to vote as established nearly a century earlier by the Fifteenth Amendment. It prohibited local and state legislatures in states with an extreme history of denying minorities the vote from passing new laws that would disenfranchise African Americans. This was accomplished by mandating that these jurisdictions submit changes in "any voting qualification...or standard, practice or procedure with respect to voting" to the U.S. attorney general's office for "preclearance." Preclearance would be granted if the Attorney General "determined that the proposed voting change did not have the purpose or the effect of denying or abridging the right to vote on account of race" (Grofman, Handley, and Niemi 1992: 17).

The Act's effect on African-American voter registration figures in these covered states was impressive. The percentage of African Americans registered to vote in the Deep South increased from 29 to 52 percent in the two years following the Act's passage. In Mississippi, black voter registration jumped from only 6 percent just prior to the Voting Rights Act to 60 percent just two years later (Grofman, Handley, and Niemi 1992). Indeed, black voter registration in Dallas County, Alabama (home of Selma) increased from 335 in 1964 to 9,000 in 1966, just one year after the Act's passage (Williams 1987).

The provisions that applied to the covered jurisdictions were meant to expire in 1970. The act was extended in 1970, 1975, and 1982, the last time for a period of 25 years. The 1975 extension significantly broadened the coverage of the Act by extending voting protection to Alaskan natives, Native Americans, Asian Americans, and Hispanics. As a result, the geographic coverage of the act was greatly expanded to areas outside the South.

Minority Vote Dilution As a Response to the Voting Rights Act

Although the Act was highly successful in guaranteeing the rights of all eligible Americans to vote, whether that vote had any value to minority group members in electing their chosen candidates to office was another matter. Following passage of the Voting Rights Act, jurisdictions throughout the South, from the Congressional level down to county school boards and city councils, changed their election procedures to ensure that new black voters would be unsuccessful at electing the candidates of their choice to office (Davidson 1989; Davidson and Grofman 1994).

Individual jurisdictions used numerous methods to dilute newly established minority voting strength. These included the use of at-large elections, in which all voters cast ballots for the entire membership of a legislative body. If most of the electorate votes exclusively for members of their own racial or ethnic group, the minority group is rarely, if ever, able to elect any candidates of its choice. As an example, consider a city with a governing council made up of 5 seats and having an election where 10 candidates, 5 supported by white voters and 5 supported by African-American voters, are running for those seats. If forty percent of the city's voters are African Americans and the remaining sixty percent are white, the five candidates supported by white voters will win all of the council's seats. African Americans, who cast two-fifths of the votes in the city, will elect no candidates of their choice.

Racial gerrymandering is another method of vote dilution. Two racial gerrymandering techniques were used to dilute minority voting strength. First, a geographically concentrated group of minority voters could be divided and parceled out among several districts, thereby making them less than fifty percent of the electorate in each district. An alternative technique was to place a large group of minority voters into a single district, so that although they may elect the candidate of their choice by an overwhelming margin in that district, the excess votes cast for the winning candidate in that district could not be used to elect candidates of the minority group's choice in surrounding districts (O'Loughlin 1982; Parker 1989; Davidson and Grofman 1994).

Minority-vote dilution techniques were used throughout the South to deny African-American voters the ability to elect the candidates of their choice, but probably the most egregious examples were found in Mississippi (Parker 1990; Morrill 1981). Inasmuch as white political leaders in Mississippi could no longer deny African Americans the right to vote, Mississippi's all-white legislature in 1966 tried to insure that those votes would have no meaning. A dozen laws were adopted aimed at diluting African-American voting strength at all levels of government and ensuring that African Americans could not elect the candidates of their choice.

Mississippi's redrawn congressional districts in the state's Delta region provide a textbook example of racial gerrymandering (Parker 1989; 1990). From 1882 to 1966, northwestern Mississippi's Delta region was the core of one congressional district. In 1960, 65 percent of the Delta district's population were African Americans. Because the vast majority of African Americans in the Delta were not allowed to register to vote, white politicians could ignore the concerns of the African-American community. With the passage of the Voting Rights Act and subsequent increases in African-American voter registration, the Delta district was on the verge of electing Mississippi's first African-American member of Congress in this century. In response, Mississippi's all-white legislature divided the Delta into three parts, with each part combined with white majority areas in eastern Mississippi. Suddenly, no district had an African-American population majority.

The state's congressional districts retained this basic configuration until the early 1980s. Not until 1984 did the Delta district re-emerge, following a lengthy series of court cases. In 1986, Mississippi's first African-American representative this century was elected to Congress.

The question was whether southern states could legally justify such egregious vote dilution. In interpreting the constitutionality of the VRA, the Supreme Court ruled in 1969 that all changes in election procedures in preclearance jurisdictions, including the type of elections used and the redrawing of district boundaries, must be submitted to the U.S. Justice Department for preclearance to insure that they do not have a discriminatory effect. This decision gave the Justice Department a powerful new tool in fighting vote dilution. In 1980, however, the Supreme Court made the successful challenge of vote dilution claims much more difficult by requiring proof of intent to discriminate. Responding to this decision, Congress, in 1982, made it easier to prove discriminatory vote dilution claims by revising and amending the VRA. According to the revised VRA, any election scheme that provided those protected by the VRA any "less opportunity than other members of the electorate...to elect representatives of their choice" was prohibited. In order to demonstrate vote dilution, challengers needed only to show evidence that the election scheme had effectively diluted their vote, whether or not such dilution was intentional.

In 1986, the United States Supreme Court provided guidance on how to demonstrate unconstitutional vote dilution under the revised VRA. In *Thornburg v. Gingles* the Court ruled that North Carolina's state legislative map had unconstitutionally diluted minority voting strength. In defending this interpretation, the Court ruled that in order to establish a case of unconstitutional vote dilution, three factors must be demonstrated: (1) that the minority group "is sufficiently large and geographically compact to constitute a majority in a single-member district;" (2) the minority group "is politically cohesive", and (3) that the "white majority votes sufficiently as a bloc to enable it...usually to defeat the minority's preferred candidate" (*Thornburg v. Gingles* at 50-51). Combined, the revised VRA and the *Gingles* decision provided an easier method for demonstrating unconstitutional cases of minority vote dilution.

Minority Representation in the 1990s

As the states prepared to redraw district boundaries after the 1990 census, the Justice Department indicated that the revised VRA would be an integral part of their preclearance strategy. That is, all redistricting plans in covered jurisdictions would be evaluated by the Justice Department to determine "whether the changes provide minority voters with the greatest feasible access to the political process" (Days 1992: 57). Rather than merely ensuring that minorities did not lose ground in representation, the Justice Department became active by aggressively ensuring

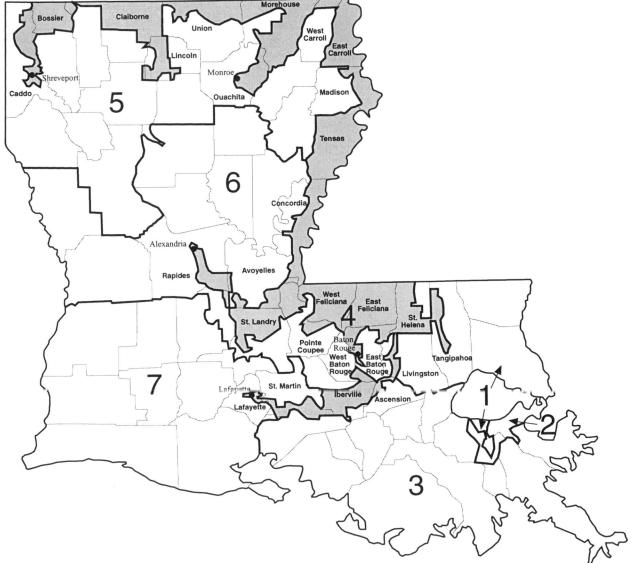

Figure 8.1. Louisiana Voting Districts 1990s

that minority groups received the maximum possible representation.

After the Census results were released in 1991, the Justice Department was vigilant in ensuring that states and localities maximized minority representation. Although the Bush administration's motives for such vigilance have been questioned, the Justice Department's actions greatly increased the number of majority-minority districts at all levels of government (that is, districts in which 50 percent or more of the voting age population were members of minority groups covered under the VRA). For example, the number of African-American and Hispanic population majority congressional districts in the U.S. doubled in the early 1990s from 26 to 52. As a result, the number of minority group members elected to public office increased substantially.

Despite these increases, both voting rights advocates and opponents have criticized the process by which the number of majority-minority districts were increased in the 1990s. Some critics argue that some majority-minority districts cut across well-recognized regional boundaries and combine disparate places, thereby ignoring traditional concepts of communities of interest (Morrill 1996). Examples include Georgia's 11th district and Louisiana's 4th district of the early 1990s (Figure 8.1). Others have argued that the maximization of majority-minority districts has carried the idea of voting rights too far and should be scrapped altogether as part of the growing tide of criticism in some circles of affirmative action-type programs and race-conscious remedies to historical and present levels of racial discrimination (e.g., Thernstrom 1987, Schmidt 1996).

Several major Supreme Court decisions examined these issues and throw into question the future of the gains achieved in minority representation in the 1990s. In the early 1990s, the Justice Department forced the state of North Carolina to create two African American-majority congressional districts. In an attempt to protect white Democratic incumbents, the state created two non-compact districts that elected North Carolina's first African-American members to Congress in this century (Pildes and Niemi 1993). Suit was brought challenging the constitutionality of the 12th district, which runs from Durham to Charlotte (Fig. 8.2). The Supreme Court, although not initially invalidating the 12th, challenged its constitutionality, arguing the district was so bizarrely shaped that "it rationally cannot be understood as anything other than an effort to segregate voters on the basis of race" (*Shaw v. Reno* at 2828).

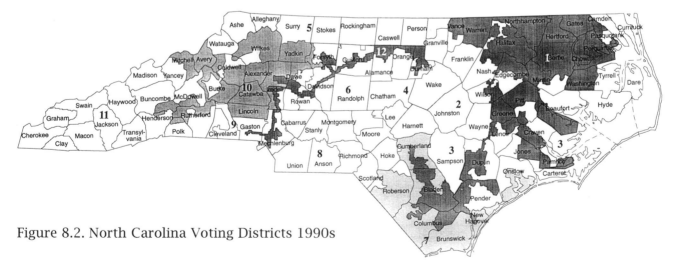

Figure 8.2. North Carolina Voting Districts 1990s

After the Court suggested that district shape could be a trigger for indicating the possibility of unconstitutional race-conscious districting, a group of Georgia voters filed suit against that state's African-American majority 11th District. This district, which had been drawn at the insistence of the Justice Department, combined a rural African-American population in middle Georgia with African-American urban populations in Augusta, Savannah, and the eastern suburbs of Atlanta. In its five-to-four decision, the Supreme Court in 1995 chastised the role of the Justice Department in forcing Georgia to create the district and ruled the district unconstitutional in part because "race was the predominant, overriding factor" in determining how the district's boundaries were drawn (*Miller v. Johnson* at 782). Both the North Carolina and Georgia cases raise important questions. What is the future of minority representation? What is the future role of the Justice Department in reviewing district plans for possible vote dilution? Should preserving communities of interest within districts be a major goal of district plans? How should these communities be defined. Should they be based on historical settlement patterns, media regions, commuting patterns, race, ethnicity, or other criteria? Will a renewed emphasis on preserving communities of interest within districts come at the expense of minority representation? What role *can* race play in devising redistricting plans aimed at helping to overcome centuries of racial discrimination?

In the near future, the Court is likely to continue to address these questions. In June 1996, the Court ruled unconstitutional two African-American majority and one Hispanic majority congressional district in Texas. At the same time, the Supreme Court also ruled unconstitutional North Carolina's 12th Congressional District, the subject of the 1993 *Shaw* ruling. This 1996 ruling in *Shaw v. Hunt* was especially significant because the Supreme Court's decision overturned a 1994 Federal District Court ruling that the 12th district was, in fact, constitutional. The District Court had agreed with the 12th district's defenders who successfully argued that as the state's only predominantly urban district the 12th was not bizarrely shaped, but rather represented a recognizable community of interest. These two Supreme Court decisions are significant because they reinforce the court's view that even if other traditional redistricting criteria play a role in drawing district lines, districts are still unconstitutional if race is *the* predominant factor in their creation.

The Supreme Court in its 1996 term heard a second case concerning congressional districts in Georgia. Following the Supreme Court's 1995 ruling in *Miller*, a Federal District Court in Georgia redrew the state's congressional district lines in *Johnson v. Miller*. Although the districts of the lower court's plan are more compact, respect county boundaries, and adhere to the state's traditional communities of interest to a greater extent than the previous plan, the lower court's plan also reduces the number of African-American population majority districts in the state from three to one. The potential effect may be the eventual elimination of two-thirds of Georgia's African-American representatives from Congress (Leib 1996). If the Supreme Court upholds the District Court's congressional lines (which as of February 1997 appears likely), the Georgia plan may be used as a blueprint for future congressional redistrictings around the country. The result will be the drawing of more compact, community of interest-oriented congressional districts, a sharp reduction in the number of majority-minority districts, and potentially a reduction in the number of minority elected officials.

Alternative Electoral Systems

Now we are left with the current situation. The Supreme Court has rejected predominantly race-conscious redistricting as it was practiced in the early 1990s, but it has given the states little guidance as to how they can accomplish non-racially discriminatory redistricting. Some have suggested other ways, however, to provide for enhanced minority representation in the political process without resorting to the strangely-shaped race conscious redistricting plans that the Supreme Court and others have increasingly come to reject (Leib and Webster 1997; Webster 1997). Among these alternatives are cumulative voting (e.g., Guinier 1994; Karlan 1989; Still and Karlan 1995; Kelly 1996). Under cumulative voting, individual voters can cast multiple votes for one candidate, or split their votes among several candidates. As a result, if members of a large-enough minority group cast all of their votes for one candidate, they can ensure the election of that candidate. To take our example of the five-member city council again, all voters get 5 votes. Under cumulative voting, voters could cast all 5 votes for one candidate, or split their votes among 2, 3, 4 or 5 different candidates. If just over one-sixth of voters cast all of their votes for one candidate, that candidate will win a seat on the council.

Advocates of cumulative voting argue that by doing away with districts and giving voters multiple votes with which they can register their *intensity* of support for candidates, the voters themselves can define their own communities of interest and vote for candidates who represent the specific community they wish to see represented, whether this community be e.g., regional, race, class, occupation, political party, or gender-based. Cumulative voting systems have been used at the local and county level in parts of Alabama, Texas, New Mexico, and South Dakota to remedy prior discriminatory electoral systems (e.g., Pildes and Donoghue 1997; Brischetto 1995).

By eliminating geographically defined districts, however, cumulative voting systems throw out centuries of place-based representation that has been a cornerstone of the American political system. Hence some cumulative voting advocates have suggested modifying these systems by dividing a jurisdiction into geographically meaningful voting regions under which they can conduct cumulative voting to send two or more representatives to the governing body.

For example, Morrill (1996; 1997) has suggested that cumulative voting could be used to elect members to the U.S. House of Representatives. Rather than having voters in each state elect all of their states' representatives, large states could be divided into regions where voters, using cumulative voting, would elect several representatives from their region to Congress who would still be responsive to the interests of their region. North Carolina, for example, could be divided into four regions, with three representatives from each elected through cumulative voting. Under a pure cumulative voting system, all voters in North Carolina would vote for all of the state's dozen representatives, which leaves the potential of having some region of the state unrepresented. Thus modified cumulative voting systems have the twin benefits of providing a better chance that members of groups long shut out from the political process receive representation, while maintaining the place-based nature of representation that was part of the founding fabric of this country.

Conclusions

For more than three centuries after the importation of the first slaves from Africa in the early 1600s, African Americans were systematically denied their civil rights in the American South. The goal of the Civil Rights Movement of the 1950s and 1960s was to achieve equal rights for African Americans for the first time in our country's history. One of the most important rights sought in order to achieve this goal was the right to vote, systematically denied to most African Americans in the South despite the enactment of the Fifteenth Amendment in 1870. The importance of the right to vote could not be overstated; as Martin Luther King, Jr. argued in his 1957 speech, "Give Us the Ballot, We Will Transform the South" (1986: 197):

> So long as I do not firmly and irrevocably possess the right to vote I do not possess myself. I cannot make up my mind—it is made up for me. I cannot live as a democratic citizen, observing the laws I have helped to enact—I can only submit to the edict of others.

The Voting Rights Act of 1965 and its later extensions were effective at providing African Americans and other minority group members with the firm and irrevocable right to vote across the United States. Since then, however, a more difficult challenge has been how to translate these votes successfully into electing candidates to office and dispersing political power to groups long shut out of the political process. In the mid 1990s, thanks to an amended and expanded Voting Rights Act, more minority group members hold public office and can wield political power than at any other time this century.

The United States is at a crossroads in terms of minority representation (see Shelley, Webster and Leib 1997). Recent actions by the U.S. Supreme Court, although aimed at making representation more geographically meaningful, are likely to lead to a diminishing of political power for minority group members. In a society that has not fully overcome three centuries of state-sanctioned discrimination despite the efforts of the past thirty years, political geographers, among others, are examining ways to provide for both geographically meaningful representation while enhancing minority representation. These issues will not be resolved quickly or easily, and will likely still be debated throughout our students' lives.

References Cited

Agnew, J. 1987. *Place and Politics: The Geographical Mediation of State and Society.* Boston: Allen & Unwin.

Brischetto, R. 1995. "Cumulative Voting as an Alternative to Districting." *National Civic Review.* 84:347-354.

Davidson, C., ed. 1989. *Minority Vote Dilution.* Washington, D.C.: Howard University Press.

Davidson, C. and B. Grofman, eds. 1994. *Quiet Revolution in the South: The Impact of the Voting Rights Act, 1965-1990.* Princeton, N. J.: Princeton University Press.

Days, D. S., III. 1992. "Section 5 and the Role of the Justice Department." Pp. 52-65 in B. Grofman and C. Davidson, eds., *Controversies in Minority Voting: The Voting Rights Act in Perspective.* Washington, D.C.: The Brookings Institution.

Garrow, D. J. 1978. *Protest at Selma: Martin Luther King, Jr., and the Voting Rights Act of 1965.* New Haven, Conn.: Yale University Press.

Geography for Life: National Geography Standards 1994. Washington, D.C.: National Geographic Research and Exploration for the American Geographical Society, Association of American Geographers, National Council for Geographic Education, and the National Geographic Society.

Grofman, B., L. Handley, and R. G. Niemi. 1992. *Minority Representation and the Quest for Voting Equality.* Cambridge, UK: Cambridge University Press.

Guinier, L. 1994. *The Tyranny of the Majority: Fundamental Fairness in Representative Democracy.* New York: Free Press.

Karlan, P. S. 1989. "Maps and Misreadings: The Role of Geographic Compactness in Racial Vote Dilution Litigation." *Harvard Civil Rights-Civil Liberties Law Review.* 24:173-248.

Kelly, L. A. 1996. "Race and Place: Geographic and Transcendent Community in the Post-Shaw Era." *Vanderbilt Law Review.* 49: 227-308.

Key, V. O. 1949. *Southern Politics in State and Nation.* New York: Knopf.

King, M. L., Jr. 1986. *A Testament of Hope: The Essential Writings of Martin Luther King, Jr.* (edited by J. M. Washington). San Francisco: Harper & Row.

Kousser, J. M. 1974. *The Shaping of Southern Politics: Suffrage Restrictions and the Establishment of the One-Party South, 1880-1910.* New Haven, Conn.: Yale University Press.

Kousser, J. M. 1992. "The Voting Rights Act and the Two Reconstructions." Pp. 135-176 in B. Grofman and C. Davidson, eds., *Controversies in Minority Voting: The Voting Rights Act in Perspective.* Washington, D.C.: The Brookings Institution.

Leib, J. I. 1996. "Redistricting and the Future of the Voting Rights Act after *Miller v. Johnson.*" Paper presented at the 92d Annual Meeting of the Association of American Geographers.

_____ and G. R. Webster. 1997. "On Enlarging the U.S. House of Representatives." *Political Geography*, 15.

Morrill, R. L. 1981. *Political Redistricting and Geographic Theory*. Washington, D.C.: Association of American Geographers.

_____.1996. "Spatial Engineering and Spatial Integrity." *Political Geography*. 15:95-98.

_____. forthcoming. "Reconciling Geography and the Politics of Race." In F. M. Shelley, G. R. Webster, and J. I. Leib, eds., *Representation, Community and Redistricting in the 1990s: A Geographic Perspective*. Syracuse, N. Y.: Syracuse University Press.

O'Loughlin, J. 1982. "The Identification and Evaluation of Racial Gerrymandering." *Annals of the Association of American Geographers*. 72: 165-184.

Parker, F. R. 1989. "Racial Gerrymandering and Legislative Reapportionment." Pp. 85-117 in C. Davidson, ed., *Minority Vote Dilution*. Washington, D.C.: Howard University Press.

_____. 1990. *Black Votes Count: Political Empowerment in Mississippi After 1965*. Chapel Hill: University of North Carolina Press.

Pildes, R. H. and K. Donoghue. forthcoming. "Cumulative Voting: A Case Study." In F. M. Shelley, G. R. Webster, and J. I. Leib, eds., *Representation, Community and Redistricting in the 1990s: A Geographic Perspective*. Syracuse, N. Y.: Syracuse University Press.

_____. and R. G. Niemi. 1993. "Expressive Harms, 'Bizarre Districts,' and Voting Rights: Evaluating Election-District Appearances after *Shaw v. Reno*." *Michigan Law Review*. 92: 483-587.

Schmidt, P. 1996. "Californians Likely to Vote This Fall on Ending Racial Preferences." *Chronicle of Higher Education*. March 1: A 34.

Shelley, F. M., J. C. Archer, F. M. Davidson, and S. D. Brunn. 1996. *Political Geography of the United States*. New York: Guilford Press.

_____, G. R. Webster, and J. I. Leib, eds. forthcoming. *Representation, Community and Redistricting in the 1990s: A Geographic Perspective*. Syracuse, N. Y.: Syracuse University Press.

Still, E. and P. Karlan. 1995. "Cumulative Voting as a Remedy in Voting Rights Cases." *National Civic Review*. 84: 337-346.

Thernstrom, A. M. 1987. *Whose Votes Count? Affirmative Action and Minority Voting Rights*. Cambridge, Mass.: Harvard University Press.

Webster, G. R. 1997. "Geography and the Decennial Task of Redistricting." *Journal of Geography*. 96: 61-68.

Williams, J. 1987. *Eyes on the Prize: America's Civil Rights Years, 1954-1965*. New York: Penguin Books.

Court Cases Cited

Johnson v. Miller, CV 194-008 United States District Court, Southern District of Georgia (1995)

Miller v. Johnson, 132 L Ed 2d 762 (1995)

Shaw v. Hunt, U.S. Supreme Court Case Number 94-923 (1996)

Shaw v. Reno, 113 S. Ct. 2816 (1993)

Thornburg v. Gingles, 478 U.S. 30 (1986)

CHAPTER 9
TEACHING ELECTORAL GEOGRAPHY
Douglas Deane Jones

The past 25 years have produced a wealth of work on the electoral geography of the United States. Electoral geography is the interpretation of mapped election results distributed across areal units. Electoral geographers examine the distribution of election outcomes across space and over time and interpret these distributions in terms of underlying social, economic, political, and cultural processes. Electoral geography research is valuable to teachers developing topical units on various aspects of the geography of the United States.

French geographer Andre Siegfried is regarded as the father of electoral geography (Taylor and Johnston 1979). Siegfried's cartographic examination of voting patterns in western France under the Third Republic is regarded as a classic geographic voting study. This study mapped the votes cast for right-wing and left-wing parties in France in the late nineteenth and early twentieth centuries. He compared maps of the distribution of party votes with maps of physical geographic features, economic activities, and social characteristics.

The well-known American historian Frederick Jackson Turner analyzed county-level voting data for the office of president over time and found that despite fluctuations in the level of support for individual presidential candidates of the same political party, the geographical pattern of support was remarkably stable over the series of elections. John Kirtland Wright (1932) reviewed presidential election results during the late nineteenth and early twentieth centuries, supporting Turner's contention that regional patterns of partisan support were generally stable over series of elections.

The purpose of this chapter is to illustrate the pedagogic value of electoral geography in the teaching of American political geography. It includes a discussion of the inherently geographical nature of the American political system, a review of recent research involving the identification of spatial and temporal trends in American presidential elections, the role of geography in campaigns and campaign strategies and the linkage between social movements and electoral geography. It then concludes with discussion of the utility of electoral analysis in teaching political geography.

The American Electoral System and Electoral Geography

The process of electing the president of the United States is inherently geographical. The United States Constitution provides for a governmental framework based explicitly on territorial representation. Members of Congress are elected from defined geographical areas, whereas the Electoral College system in the Constitution is designed in such a way that winning the popular vote is neither necessary nor sufficient for election to the Presidency.

Each state's number of votes in the Electoral College equals its membership in both houses of Congress (see also Webster 1997). For example, Texas has 30 members in the House of Representatives plus two Senators, giving the state 32 votes in the Electoral College. In most states, all the electoral votes are cast for the candidate winning the largest number of votes in the state. Maine and Nebraska have recently enacted a slight modification to the statewide winner-take-all system. In these two states, the winner in each congressional district is entitled to one Electoral College vote with the two remaining votes awarded to the statewide winner. The candidate winning a majority of votes in the Electoral College, at present a total of 270 electoral votes, wins the presidency.

In planning a campaign strategy, party officials recognize that the Electoral College system implies that a presidential election is, in effect, fifty-one separate elections—one in each of the fifty states and one in the District of Columbia. To win the presidency, a candidate must achieve pluralities in enough states to win a total of 270 electoral votes. It is possible, therefore, for a candidate to win the most popular votes nationwide but lose the election in the Electoral College, although this has not happened since 1888 when Benjamin Harrison defeated Grover Cleveland despite Cleveland winning some 100,000 more popular votes.

These considerations imply that geographical variations in support for political parties are important. Each presidential campaign spends considerable time, money, and effort to develop strategies that will allow it to stitch together a winning combination of states to produce a majority in the Electoral College (Archer and Shelley 1986).

Identifying Electoral Regions in the United States

Over the last quarter century, geographers have been active in trying to identify the distinctive regional patterns of support for the two major political parties. Generally, the political landscape of America has been anchored by the view of southern distinctiveness. The term Solid South came into widespread usage among academicians and journalists to describe the Democratic party's political dominance of the region.

Because the South was dependably Democratic, it was generally ignored in presidential elections. Seldom was a Southerner seriously considered for a major-party presidential or vice-presidential nomination. Instead, the Republicans tried to win enough electoral votes in the Northeast, Midwest, and West to overcome Democratic dominance in the South. The Democrats, meanwhile, made efforts to pry enough Northern or Western states away from the Republicans to ensure an Electoral College majority, although only Grover Cleveland, Woodrow Wilson, and Franklin Delano Roosevelt succeeded in doing so between 1868 and 1944.

Since the end of World War II, however, the South has become politically volatile and consequently politically powerful (Black and Black 1992; Shelley and Archer 1995). Not since the 1920s has a candidate been elected to the presidency without carrying a significant number of Southern states in the Electoral College. The post-World War II transformation of Southern politics has been linked to the increasingly leftward orientation of the Democratic Party nationwide, especially in the area of civil rights. The Thurmond and Wallace revolts of 1948 and 1968 over the Democratic party's civil rights agenda, along with the large increase in African-American voter registration following the Voting Rights Act of 1965 signaled the beginnings of a new era in southern regional politics.

Demographic changes have also contributed to the political transformation of the South. Urbanization was cited as a potential threat to the long dominance of the Democratic party in the South by the eminent political scientist V. O. Key, Jr. as early as 1949. Key (1949) argued that growth of urban business interests that shared Republican economic philosophy combined with the further leftward veering of the Democratic party nationally could eventually undermine Democratic loyalties.

Over the past three decades, the only Democratic Party presidential nominees to win substantial Electoral College support in the South were themselves Southerners (Lyndon Johnson of Texas, Jimmy Carter of Georgia, and Bill Clinton of Arkansas). Brunn and Ingalls (1972) explored the emergence of Republican voting strength within the urban South. They found that high levels of Republican support first came from counties with the largest cities. Over successive elections, GOP support gradually moved down the urban hierarchy into counties with smaller populations.

Migration of whites into the South has contributed to the growth of Republican strength in the region (Black and Black 1992). The long term political changes that have occurred in the South can be placed in a larger perspective by comparing the South to other regions of the United States. An important new avenue of research on the geography of voting is identifying and analyzing historical change in the pattern of electoral support. Archer and Taylor (1981) spurred this line of research, which used factor analysis to identify distinctive electoral regions and epochs in American presidential election history.

Factor analysis can be used to identify critical elections and electoral regions. "The purpose of T-mode analysis is identification of clusters of elections [that] correspond with electoral epochs. In S-mode analysis the emphasis is identification of clusters of states [that] correspond with electoral regions or sections (Archer and Shelley 1986: 48)." In examining state-level voting returns from 1872 through 1980, Archer and Taylor (1981) identified three distinctive voting regions—the South, the Northeast, and the West. These regions are clearly associated with the global economy.

This regionalization of the American polity has been interpreted in terms of the changing politi-cal-economic relationships of the three sections to one another (Archer et al. 1988; Shelley et al. 1996).

Section and Party (Archer and Taylor 1981) spurred a string of research articles extending the analysis over subsequent elections and investigating patterns within subnational regions (Archer et al. 1988; Shelley and Archer 1984, 1989, 1994, 1995). Further, the framework of electoral regions identified in Section and Party have been employed to investigate other aspects of American pres-idential electoral geography. For example, Murauskas et al. (1988) explored whether electoral regions or urban-suburban-rural status is more important in explaining the variance in presiden-tial party voting levels across the country. They found that distinctions between urban, suburban, and rural counties varied substantially across the three sections: "[Although] urban counties have generally been more supportive of Democratic presidential candidates than rural or suburban counties in the Northeast and West, stronger Democratic support has become more of a rural phe-nomenon in the South" (Murauskas et al. 1988: 81). Sectionalism is more important in accounting for voting patterns than urban status. Yet urban status plays a role in accounting for differences in the distribution of voting patterns between regional sections.

The Geography of Election Campaigns

Political strategists are undoubtedly aware of long-run electoral patterns such as those identified in the literature discussed above. Because the electoral process itself is so closely linked to geog-raphy, and because *where* votes are cast can be as important as *how many* are cast for a particu-lar party or candidate, political strategy has a decidedly geographical focus.

Several recent examples illustrate the importance of geography to political strategy in U.S. Presidential elections. During the 1980s, for example, concern among Southern political leaders that the South had insufficient influence in the selection of Presidential nominees led to agreement among several Southern states to hold primary elections on the same day, Super Tuesday. In 1992, success in the Super Tuesday primary states was instrumental in propelling Bill Clinton to the Democratic Party nomination. Once nominated, Clinton concentrated his campaign in the Great Lakes states and the South. The routes of his well-documented bus tours across these regions illus-trated the importance of geography to the ultimately successful Democratic Party strategy.

Brunn (1974) mapped the Democratic and Republican presidential and vice-presidential tickets for all presidential elections from 1900 to 1972. His maps illustrate that the two parties have employed vastly different spatial strategies, and these differences continued through the 1996 election. The Republicans have had a Californian on their ticket in 11 out of the last 25 elections, winning seven of these 11 elections. In contrast, the Democrats have never nominated a presiden-tial or vice-presidential candidate from west of the Rocky Mountains.

We can also see a difference in strategy by examining presidential election campaign stops. Critics of Republican Richard Nixon's unsuccessful race for the Presidency against John Kennedy in 1960 have argued that Nixon's promise to campaign in all fifty states may have been instru-mental in contributing to his narrow defeat. The time and effort spent in visiting small and remote destinations such as Alaska, Hawaii, and Montana might better have been spent in campaigning in larger states such as Illinois or Texas, which Nixon barely lost. As small states in the South have become more dependably Republican, however, this difference may disappear. Rather, both par-ties are concentrating their resources on large states with substantial Electoral College represen-tation.

Electoral Geography and Social Movements

The development of social movements provides an opportunity to explore important questions (see Cope 1997; and on environmental issues see Steinberg (1997) and Chapter 12 by Solecki and Birnbaum in this volume). American political ideology channels social movements onto the elec-toral stage. American history is replete with examples of social movements that have become integrated into the fabric of American electoral geography. As new issues arise, political parties come to be identified with positions on these issues. During the nineteenth century, for example, the Republican Party itself became established in the North as an outgrowth of the abolitionist movement. Linking support for the abolition of slavery to the industrialization of the Northeast, the Republicans soon achieved major-party status.

During the late nineteenth century, several agrarian protest or populist movements arose in the Great Plains and the West in response to a perception that industrial interests were responsible for policies resulting in increased economic hardship for the farmer. In the 1890s, the People's or Populist Party emerged in this region as a third-party alternative to the conservative economic policies of Republicans and Democrats alike. In 1896, the Populists fused with the Democrats, placing the radical agenda of the Populists squarely before the electorate. Although the Democrat-Populist coalition failed to achieve the presidency, many of the policies advocated by the Populists, including regulation of banks and securities, a progressive income tax, and the use of the secret ballot in elections, became law during the early twentieth century.

The civil rights movements by African Americans and the anti-Vietnam War movement of the 1960s provided inspiration for other groups to push for social change through a variety of methods including electoral means. Hispanics, Native Americans, gay rights advocates, and various evangelical Christian organizations are among groups that have been active in recent social movements.

Issues of social identity and societal values have become the subject of voter-initiated ballot propositions in several states. Efforts to codify the prohibition of discrimination on the basis of sexual orientation and reactions against such efforts have been occurring at the local and state level in several states. Social identity and societal values are also at the heart of the language controversy surrounding the establishment of Official English and English Only policies being promoted across the United States. Geographers are making contributions in understanding the dynamics of the political conflict.

State iconography also provides a window for understanding social movement struggles. Leib (1995) documents the political backlash against the growing civil rights movements by the Georgia legislature in 1965 to create a new state flag incorporating the Confederate battle flag within the design. The struggle over the symbolism of past discrimination represented by the Confederate battle flag continues today. Legislative votes regarding state iconography not only contribute to illuminating the cultural and social geography of the state but also enrich the understanding of social movements or the backlash resistance to social movements.

Conclusion

Mapped analysis of election returns has considerable utility to teaching political geography. Election maps are not only easy to prepare and interpret but they provide the student with a valuable tool by which they can understand social, economic, and political processes that underlie geographic differences in electoral outcomes.

National Geography Standard 13 calls attention to the dual role of conflict and cooperation in understanding political geography (*Geography for Life* 1994: 90-91, 130-131, 169-170, 210-211). Elections are a form of conflict, yet in the United States and other countries the electoral system provides for orderly transfer of power and hence provides an underlying structure of cooperation. The examples in this paper illustrate the utility of electoral geography and electoral mapping in teaching political geography.

References Cited

Archer, J. C., G. T. Murauskas, F. M. Shelley, P. J. Taylor, E. R. White 1985. "Counties, States, Sections and Parties in the 1984 Presidential Election," *Professional Geographer*, 37: 279-287.

_____ ., and F. M. Shelley 1986. *American Electoral Mosaics.* Washington, D.C.: Association of American Geographers.

_____ ., F. M. Shelley, P. J. Taylor, and E. R. White 1988. "The Geography of U.S. Presidential Elections," *Scientific American,* 259: 18-25.

_____ ., and P. J. Taylor 1981. *Section and Party.* New York: Wiley.

Black, E., and M. Black, 1992. *The Vital South: How Presidents Are Elected.* Cambridge, Massachusetts: Harvard University Press.

Brunn, S. D. 1974. *Geography and Politics in America.* New York: Harper and Row.

_____ . and G. Ingalls 1972. "The Emergence of Republicanism in the Urban South," *Southeastern Geographer,* 12: 133-144.

Cope, M. 1997. "Participation, Power, and Policy: Developing a Gender-Sensitive Political Geography," *Journal of Geography,* 96: 91-97.

Key, V. O. 1949. *Southern Politics.* New York: Random House.

Leib, J. I. 1995. "Heritage Versus Hate: A Geographical Analysis of Georgia's Confederate Battle Flag Debate," *Southeastern Geographer,* 35: 37-57.

Murauskas, G. T., J. C. Archer, and F. M. Shelley 1988. "Metropolitan, Nonmetropolitan, and Sectional Variations in Voting Behavior in Recent Presidential Elections," *Western Political Quarterly,* 41: 63-84.

Shelley, F. M. and J. C. Archer 1989. "Sectionalism and Presidential Politics in America: A Twentieth Century Reinvestigation of Voting Patterns in Illinois, Indiana and Ohio," *Journal of Interdisciplinary History,* 20: 227-255.

_____ and J. C. Archer 1994. "Some Geographical Aspects of the 1992 American Presidential Election," *Political Geography,* 13: 137-159.

_____ and 1995. "The Volatile South: A Historical Geography of Presidential Elections in the South," *Southeastern Geographer,* 35: 22-36.

_____ , J. C. Archer, F. M. Davidson, and S. D. Brunn 1996. *The Political Geography of the United States.* New York: Guilford Press.

Steinberg, P. E. 1997. "Political Geography and the Environment," *Journal of Geography,* 96: 113-118.

Taylor, P. J., and R. J. Johnston 1979. *Geography of Elections.* New York: Holmes and Meier.

Webster, G. R. 1997. "Geography and the Decennial Task of Redistricting," *Journal of Geography,* 96: 61-68.

Wright, J. K. 1932. "Voting Habits in the United States: A Note on Two Maps," *Geographical Review,* 22: 666-672.

CHAPTER 10

TEACHING THE GEOGRAPHY OF UNITED STATES FOREIGN POLICY

Fred M. Shelley

National Geography Standard 13 in *Geography for Life* (1994) calls attention to the importance of cooperation and conflict in the study of political geography. These themes are examined at a variety of spatial scales. Investigations of international political geography examine cooperation and conflict between countries, whereas other political geographers examine cooperation and conflict within countries, regions, or localities. Relatively less attention has been paid, however, to the themes of cooperation and conflict as applied to debates within countries involving foreign policy issues.

In 1900, the United States had emerged as a world power for the first time in its history. Half a century later, the United States had become the dominant power in global politics. Today, continuing changes in the global economy have encouraged many to question whether the United States will remain the leading political and economic power in the world.

Throughout American history, foreign affairs have often influenced and in turn been influenced by domestic politics. The interface between domestic politics and foreign affairs provides a rich source of information to the teacher of political geography. Examination of these issues can provide an often fascinating and controversial window on the past and the present, as well as a perspective on the future. The purpose of this chapter is twofold: to examine the interface between United States foreign and domestic policy from a political-geographic perspective emphasizing the changing role of the United States within the world economy, and to illustrate how this perspective provides a source of information for teachers and students in political geography who wish to encourage increased awareness of relationships between the United States and the world economy.

American Geopolitics

The study of geographic influences on international relations and political conflicts—a subject long central to political geography—is known as geopolitics. During the nineteenth and twentieth centuries, scholars and political leaders in various countries developed systematic analyses of their countries' changing geopolitical positions. In most cases, such geopolitical analyses were linked closely to the development of foreign policy in their respective countries.

What are the basic underpinnings of American geopolitics? Four major concerns have underlain U.S. geopolitics over the course of the twentieth century (Parker 1985; Shelley *et al.* 1996). These include dominance over the Western Hemisphere, domination of air and space, control over the Arctic, and tension between isolationism and interventionism. In 1823, President James Monroe announced what became known as the Monroe Doctrine. The Monroe Doctrine asserted that the United States would actively oppose any European attempt to reassert control over the Western Hemisphere. Opposition to European interference in the Western Hemisphere has remained a cornerstone of American geopolitics ever since.

During the nineteenth century, the Atlantic Ocean separated the United States from Europe by more than three thousand miles. Not only was the United States able to develop without interference from the European powers but it was able to develop without active involvement in European affairs. Once the airplane was invented, however, the world shrank dramatically. The United States, in effect, was now closer than ever to Europe. During World War II, the editors of *Fortune* commented that "[w]hoever controls the main strategic postwar air bases, together with the technical facilities to keep them manned, will unquestionably be the world's strongest power (Weigert and Stefansson 1944: 121)."

Because the shortest air distance between two places is the great-circle route that extends across the Arctic region, American geopolitical thought has also emphasized control of the Arctic region. Some American geopolitical thinkers have called the Arctic the "American Mediterranean" (Stefansson 1922). During the Cold War, American foreign policy emphasized cultivating friendly relations with Canada and the Scandinavian countries as well as maintaining a series of military bases along the Arctic from Alaska to Iceland and Scandinavia.

A fourth fundamental tenet of U.S. geopolitics has been ongoing tension between two alternative perspectives concerning the United States' role in the world economy. These perspectives are referred to as isolationism and internationalism. Proponents of isolationism have argued the United States should not take an active role in foreign affairs, whereas supporters of internationalism argue for a more assertive role for the United States in the international community.

Tension between isolationism and internationalism in the United States is characterized by ongoing temporal and geographic dimensions. Historians have pointed out that the relative importance of isolationism and internationalism has oscillated in cycles of approximately twenty to thirty years throughout United States history (Klingberg 1983; Schlesinger 1986; Goldstein 1988). According to this view, cycles dominated by the isolationist perspective are called introvert cycles, whereas those dominated by an internationalist perspective are known as extrovert cycles.

Four extrovert cycles, each followed by an introvert cycle, can be identified. During introvert cycles, the percentage of Federal government outlays devoted to defense-related activities has dropped substantially. During extrovert cycles, on the other hand, a much higher proportion of Federal revenues has been devoted to military and defense-related expenditures (Shelley *et al.* 1996, Chapter 7).

The Changing Geography of U.S. Foreign Policy

At any given point in time, support for internationalism has also varied geographically. Geographical variation in levels of support for activism in United States foreign policy has been evident since the United States first became an independent country.

In the nineteenth century, for example, the South and the West supported the Louisiana Purchase and the Northeast opposed it. Similarly, New Englanders opposed the Mexican War and the annexation of Texas on the grounds that the resulting annexation of territory would provide the South with the opportunity to expand slavery into new territories.

By the early twentieth century, the now-industrialized Northeast and the export-oriented South had become increasingly concerned with the establishment and maintenance of overseas economic connections. Middle Western agricultural products, on the other hand, were for the most part consumed within the United States. The Northeast and the South, therefore, tended to adopt an extrovert or internationalist outlook on many foreign policy issues, whereas persons in the Middle West tended to espouse an introvert or isolationist view.

Immigration patterns also contributed to local attitudes toward foreign policy. Areas with substantial numbers of Irish-Americans and German-Americans such as Boston and Milwaukee tended to contain large numbers of isolationists. Isolationism in these communities reflected the fact that many United States foreign policy initiatives involved support for Britain, especially before the United States entered World Wars I and II. Both before and after World War II, "[t]he Midwest and West clashed with states from the Atlantic seaboard, the Gulf Coast and the Pacific Rim over the White House's efforts to centralize foreign policy-making power and to stimulate and regulate American involvement in the world economy" (Trubowitz 1992: 175). In 1939, for example, a *Fortune* magazine survey revealed that 39.6 percent of Americans believed that the United States should sell no armaments to foreign countries. This percentage varied, however, from 29.7 percent in the Southwest to 53.7 percent in the Northern Plains states (Shelley *et al.* 1996).

After World War II, the pattern of internationalism in the East and South and isolationism in the interior persisted for more than two decades. Trubowitz (1992: 177) has shown that support for what he terms Cold War internationalism—that is, support for "bills designed to promote an open, interdependent world economy and isolate or 'contain' the Soviet bloc" was greatest in the South and the Northeast during the Cold War, while opposition was concentrated in the Middle West. The geography of foreign policy began to change during the late 1960s, as the United States became increasingly involved in Vietnam. As Trubowitz (1992: 183) has put it, "The coastal-interior axis of conflict underlying debates over American foreign policy during the height of the Cold War in the late 1940s and early 1950s [had become] a thing of the past."

Instead, foreign policy debates began to occur along a Rustbelt-Sunbelt axis, with the North isolationist and the Sunbelt internationalist.

The Sunbelt, which by the 1960s had emerged as the fastest-growing region of the United States, owed much of its growth to military and defense-related activities. Throughout the Cold War, industrial growth in the Sunbelt was reinforced by expanded governmental and private-sector spending associated with the Cold War itself (Bluestone and Harrison 1982; Markusen *et al.* 1991). Indeed, the term Gunbelt or Defense Perimeter has been applied to those areas of the United States that have benefited from military activities associated with the Cold War. Meanwhile, the traditional manufacturing core of the United States, or the Rustbelt, was losing large numbers of jobs to the Sunbelt and to foreign countries. These considerations induced Rustbelt representatives to call for more protection and isolationism, whereas the Sunbelt called for free trade and strong national defense.

The Geography of Free Trade

Analogous to the ongoing debate between isolationism and intervention is a long-standing conflict between supporters and opponents of free trade between the United States and other countries. Since the end of the Cold War, this debate often has been acrimonious because of the argument that international trade considerations may increasingly shape international geopolitics in the post-Cold War era (Chapter 11 addresses analogous issues from a Canadian point of view).

The debate concerning trade-related issues has long revolved around whether the United States should impose protective tariffs, or taxes on the import of foreign goods. Historically, Northeastern industrial interests have advocated high tariffs to protect American industry from foreign competition. On the other hand, Southerners dependent on the sale of cotton and other agricultural products overseas supported free trade. Whereas the Northeast and the South tended to agree on the desirability of foreign policy intervention, their interests have diverged with respect to the free trade issue. Republicans, who were generally supported by Northeastern industrialists, tended to support protectionism whereas Democrats tended to support free trade.

The traditional geography of protectionism is evident from the distribution of votes in the House of Representatives on various protective tariffs between the 1920s and the 1950s (Smith and Hart 1955). The West and the Northeast strongly supported high protective tariffs, whereas the South voted against them. Since the 1960s, however, the historical positions of the two major parties on free trade have reversed themselves. Many Democrats, especially in the Rustbelt, have supported protective tariffs whereas Republicans have supported free trade.

In 1987, the House of Representatives narrowly passed the Gephardt Amendment to the Omnibus Trade Act of 1988. The Gephardt Amendment would have required countries with a large trade surplus to cut surpluses voluntary or be assigned quotas or tariffs to rectify trade imbalances (Wade and Gates 1990). Most House members voted along party lines. Only 18 of 159 Republicans supported it, and all but two of these Republicans represented districts in the Northeast. On the other hand, only 55 of 255 Democrats voted against the amendment. Forty-five of these 55 Democrats who opposed the Gephardt Amendment came from the South or the West.

This fundamental change in the geography of free trade support was even more evident in the distribution of support for the North American Free Trade Agreement (NAFTA) bill of 1993. NAFTA had been proposed originally by Republicans Presidents Ronald Reagan and George Bush. In 1993, however, Democratic President Bill Clinton emerged as a key supporter of NAFTA. Many Congressional Democrats argued against NAFTA, whereas some Republican leaders emerged as key supporters. For the most part, Democrats from the Northeast and Midwest strongly opposed NAFTA. Republicans throughout the country were more prone to support NAFTA.

The distribution of support across the two major parties varied substantially by region. In the South, 54 of 86 Democrats supported NAFTA, as did 36 of 54 Republicans. In contrast, Representatives from outside the South were sharply divided along partisan lines. Northeastern

Democrats rejected the NAFTA bill by an 85-17 margin. Northeastern Republicans, on the other hand, strongly supported NAFTA. In the Great Lakes region, 34 of 39 Republican Representatives voted for the bill. Among Western Democrats, NAFTA was supported by a narrow majority, but a large majority of Republicans from the West supported it.

The Changing Geography of United States Foreign Policy
The examples presented in the preceding discussion illustrate the importance of place and location to the understanding of why persons in different areas support or oppose various policy initiatives involving relationships between the United States and other countries. How might levels of support for foreign and trade policy initiatives change in the future? How can speculation about such changes be used in teaching political geography?

To a considerable extent, efforts to address such questions can be linked to the end of the Cold War. The Chapters by Blouet (2), Davidson (4), Brunn (5), and Rechlin Perkins (13) in this volume have examined how the end of the Cold War has affected the political map of Europe. Even though the political map of the United States has not changed, the end of the Cold War has had substantial effects on U.S. foreign policy.

Markusen and Yudken (1992: 1) stated that "Ever since the Depression, preparing for warfare has been a permanent and potent American preoccupation. Consuming considerable human, financial and public-sector resources, a military-oriented economy is and has been the industrial policy of the United States." During the Cold War period, high levels of government expenditure on research and development for military purposes were frequently justified on the basis that they would also result in the development of products of value to civilians. By the 1980s, however, it had become evident that government expenditures on military-related activities were less beneficial to the civilian economy than had been assumed previously. Dollars spent on civilian goods in effect flow farther through the domestic economy than do those spent on military items. The term peace dividend was coined in order to reflect the potentially greater effect of civilian expenditures on economic growth within the United States.

Despite the peace dividend, any efforts to convert production from military to civilian orientation is likely to result in some significant short-term effects on local communities. Crump and Archer (1993) have pointed out that post-Cold War federal expenditures are likely to be distributed more evenly than in the past, since domestic outlays tend to be allocated on a more geographically uniform basis than defense outlays. Gunbelt communities, on the other hand, may suffer adverse effects from reduced military and defense-related expenditures.

This point is evident in the recent debate over closing military bases. Since the end of the Cold War, U.S. government policy has been oriented to reducing the size of U.S. military forces. Yet military expenditures are highly concentrated geographically. In many communities, military bases are important employers, not only of military personnel but also of civilian employees. For example, Tinker Air Force Base near Oklahoma City is the largest single-site employer in the entire state of Oklahoma. Moreover, the presence of a military base creates numerous jobs for teachers, physicians, merchants, and other persons who work in businesses providing services to military personnel and their dependents. The closure of a military base could have profound effects on large numbers of civilian employees and their families.

In light of these considerations, the considerable potential for political deadlock in the face of opposing national and local interests led to adoption of the Defense Base Closure and Realignment Act of 1990. This law established an elaborate base-closing procedure. The responsibility for choosing specific military facilities to be closed is delegated to a blue-ribbon Defense Base Closure and Realignment Commission. Members of the Commission are collectively charged with preparing and presenting a list of bases slated for closure to the Secretary of Defense, who in turn is expected to transmit the list to the President. The President may either return the list to the Commission for reconsideration, or may submit the entire list to Congress. Congress has the choice between approving or disapproving the list in its entirety, without floor amendments to add or subtract bases from the list. This all-or-nothing approach clearly was designed to insulate members of Congress from the wrath of angered constituents in affected areas (Shelley et al. 1996).

Like other communities, present or former military-industrial complex communities maintain urban growth machines (Logan and Molotch 1976). Local government and business leaders cooperate in order to promote industrial expansion and urban growth. In doing so, communities will have to adjust in response to the new world order. No longer are communities likely to identify dependence on the military-industrial complex as a means to growth and development. Rather, the development of stronger parallels between the world economy and the global political system suggests that the activities of an urban growth machine may focus more directly on those activities that promote international trade and circulation. For example, cities such as Miami, Los Angeles, and Seattle are apt to benefit from their locations with respect to the geographically broad-scale trading horizons of the Caribbean and the Pacific Rim.

The debate over the merits of NAFTA highlighted the common belief that the post-Cold War world will emphasize an accelerated level of international trade. Many NAFTA advocates suggested that the development of a free-trade zone within North America would be critical to American efforts to compete with the growing economies of Japan and Western Europe. Indeed, NAFTA advocates frequently cited the European Community as a model for international cooperation underlain by free trade. On this view, failure to enact NAFTA could seriously hinder American efforts to compete in a post-Cold War global economy.

At the same time, many on both sides of the NAFTA debate expressed specific concern about particular communities within the United States. The underlying ambivalence is evident from a brief examination of the debates within the House during the several days before the passage of the NAFTA bill. Both sides recognized that the costs associated with the implementation of NAFTA were likely to be concentrated geographically, whereas potential benefits were distributed more evenly over larger areas.

Both supporters and opponents of NAFTA called attention to the potential effects of NAFTA on local areas. Members of Congress from such cities as San Antonio, El Paso, and San Diego emerged as key supporters of the bill. For example, Representative Ron Packard of California stated in a Congressional debate that "NAFTA is key to San Diego's vision of the future. Because of the city's unique resources and position, it will become a gateway to emerging international markets" (*Congressional Record*, November 10, 1993: E2815). Analogous arguments were articulated in opposition to NAFTA by representatives from working-class, blue-collar districts in the Northeast and the Great Lakes states. This was parallel to the anti-free trade arguments made by Canadian opponents as articulated in Chapter 11.

Central to many of these anti-NAFTA arguments was concern for the decline of American values, as represented by the farmer, the small businessperson, and the worker. Much of the opposition to NAFTA involved concern that such individuals would be swallowed up by the forces of bigness and bureaucracy such as large multinational corporations, agribusiness, and large retail corporations.

Rural opposition to bigness and bureaucracy may also be evident in other contemporary foreign policy debates. In mid-1994, for example, the Clinton Administration proposed to send American troops to Haiti to restore the government of that country's elected President, Jean-Bertrand Aristide. Clinton's proposal was most strongly opposed in the interior regions, and supported along the Eastern seaboard. Support for foreign policy activism may increasingly be related to attitudes toward immigration. A successful American invasion of Haiti was seen to reduce the flow of Haitian immigrants to the United States, the large majority of whom settle in Florida and in the large cities of the Eastern Seaboard. Similarly, NAFTA supporters in California and Texas pointed to the possibility that improved economic conditions in Mexico would discourage Mexicans from moving to their states.

Conclusion

The examples presented in this chapter illustrate that the interface between foreign and domestic policy has an explicitly geographic dimension. Throughout American history, disagreement over foreign policy has been carried out in both houses of Congress and in the ballot box. In particular, conflict within the American polity over foreign policy has involved ongoing tension between advocates of isolation and those of intervention. The different positions of various regions of the United States within the global economy help to explain ongoing patterns of support and opposition for foreign policy initiatives. At the same time, most Americans have tended to cooperate in support of the major concerns of American geopolitics.

Undoubtedly, the geography of attitudes and policy positions concerning American foreign policy will come into sharper focus with the passage of time and the march of international events. Examining foreign policy initiatives and their different effects on various parts of the United States provides a valuable method of reinforcing the dual themes of cooperation and conflict as emphasized in Standard 13.

References Cited

Bluestone, B., and B. Harrison 1982. *The Deindustrialization of America: Plant Closings, Community Abandonment and the Dismantling of Basic Industry*. New York: Basic Books.

Crump, J. R., and J. C. Archer 1993. "Spatial and Temporal Variability in the Geography of American Defense Outlays," *Political Geography*, 12: 38-63.

Goldstein, J. S. 1988. *Long Cycles: Prosperity and War in the Modern Age*. New Haven: Yale University Press.

Klingberg, F. L. 1983. *Cyclical Trends in American Foreign Policy Moods: The Unfolding of America's World Role*. Lanham, Maryland: University Press of America.

Logan, J. R., and H. L. Molotch 1976. Urban Fortunes: *The Political Economy of Place*. Berkeley: University of California Press.

Markusen, A., P. Hall, S. Campbell, and S. Deitrick 1991. *The Rise of the Gunbelt: The Military Remapping of Industrial America*. New York: Oxford.

_____, and J. Yudken 1992. *Dismantling the Cold War Economy*. New York: Basic Books.

Parker, G. J. 1985. *Western Geopolitical Thought in the Twentieth Century*. London: Croom Helm.

Schlesinger, A., Jr. 1986. *Cycles of American History*. Boston: Houghton Mifflin.

Shelley, F. M., J. C. Archer, F. M. Davidson, and S. D. Brunn 1996. *The Political Geography of the United States*. New York: Guilford.

Smith, H. R., and J. F. Hart 1955. "The American Tariff Map," *Geographical Review*, 45: 327-346.

Stefansson, V. 1922. *The Northward Course of Empire*. New York: Harcourt Brace.

Trubowitz, P. 1992, "Sectionalism and American Foreign Policy: The Political Geography of Consensus and Conflict," *International Studies Quarterly*, 36: 173-190.

Wade, L. L., and J. B. Gates 1990. "A New Tariff Map of the United States (House of Representatives)," Political Geography Quarterly, 9: 284-304.

Weigert, H. W., and V. Stefansson (eds.) 1944. Compass of the World: A Symposium on Political Geography. New York: Macmillan.

Part III. Global Perspectives

CHAPTER 11

THE RHETORIC AND RATIONALE OF FREE TRADE: A POLITICAL GEOGRAPHY PERSPECTIVE

Christopher D. Merrett

The National Geography Standards challenge geographers to explain "how the forces of cooperation and conflict among people influence the division and control of the Earth's surface" (*Geography for Life* 1994: 130). The globalization of capital manifested in free trade agreements represents a powerful force influencing the division and control of the earth's surface (Harvey 1982; Lipietz 1987; Knox and Agnew 1989). Yet we are hard pressed to predict and then explain what the consequences of free trade will be for the countries involved in free trade agreements. Something called free trade appears to offer universal benefits to all who partake of it. Yet we all know the old adage: "there is no such thing as a free lunch." Can we also say that there is no such thing as free trade? Do some regions and economic sectors benefit at the expense of others under free trade? Political geographers can hope only to explain the effects of free trade if they clearly understand the assumptions that underlie arguments for and against free trade agreements.

The North American Free Trade Agreement, which was ratified by the United States Congress in the fall of 1993, was front-page news across the United States. Earlier, however, negotiations leading up to the implementation of the Canada-United States Free Trade Agreement (FTA) in January 1989 received scant attention by most Americans. Although few Americans were aware of the issue, the issue of free trade between Canada and the United States was debated vigorously by Canadians. Proponents of the FTA predicted that few jobs would leave Canada and that free trade would prompt only a reallocation of resources within Canada. Opponents, on the other hand, believed that investment capital and many manufacturing jobs would leave Canada as tariffs were lowered. Canadian manufacturers and American branch-plants located in Canada would move to lower-cost production regions such as the American Southeast where unions are weak and wages are low.

This chapter compares the arguments used to support or oppose free trade prior to the implementation of the FTA in 1989 with its consequences six years later. It proceeds in the following manner. First, it outlines the assumptions and predictions made by supporters and opponents to free trade. Second, it presents some of the consequences of free trade. Third, it provides some conclusions about the effects of free trade. Fourth, it outlines an exercise for learning about free trade.

Predictions about the Effects of Free Trade

Free trade supporters relied on the neoclassical model of free trade first developed by two British economists, Adam Smith and David Ricardo. Smith and Ricardo argued that free trade was beneficial to all trading partners. Smith argued that economic growth was the key to national wealth and power. When countries impeded economic growth by erecting barriers against the exchange of goods, their domestic welfare and economic growth would suffer from protectionist strategies. Smith also argued that countries should specialize to produce the best goods possible based upon their national resource endowment and then engage in free trade with other countries to become wealthy and powerful. Smith's trade theory, therefore, was based on the merits of a territorial division of labor and *absolute advantage* in production.

In 1817, Ricardo extended Smith's theory to establish the law of *comparative advantage* as the fundamental rationale for free trade. Smith had assumed that the wealth of two trading partners would be maximized if each country specialized to produce goods in which it has the greatest efficiency. Both countries can maximize prosperity if they specialize to produce commodities in which they have an absolute advantage and trade with each other. What happens to the country that enjoys no absolute advantage in the production of any commodity? Ricardo demonstrated that both countries should still engage in trade because the flow of goods between countries is determined by the comparative, not absolute, costs of the goods produced. When a country enjoys an absolute advantage over another in the production of two commodities, it should specialize in the production of that good for which it has the greatest comparative advantage and leave the production of other commodities to other countries. The creation of an international division of labor enables all countries to gain more from exchange. This simple yet elegant idea based on comparative advantage and the universal benefits of specialization remains a central tenet of neoclassical free trade theory.

As Canadians began to consider the merits of the FTA, the Economic Council of Canada (ECC) used neoclassical assumptions to predict that the FTA would generate three new jobs for every one lost. The ECC also predicted that the FTA would create 250,000 new jobs for Canadians between 1989 and 1998. Furthermore, Canada's industrial sector would expand because of specialization, economies of scale, and access to the American market which was larger than the Canadian market by a factor of ten.

Canadian academic economists also promoted free trade based on neoclassical models. Harris and Cox (1984) concluded that jobs would increase in all sectors except primary products. A document signed by 250 Canadian economists, submitted to a House of Commons legislative committee hearing, stated that the FTA would provide better investment opportunities, a higher standard of living, lower-cost commodities, and a greater diversity of products for Canadians than under the current policy (Tremblay 1988). Wonnacott and Hill (1987) predicted that few if any American branch-plants or Canadian firms would relocate jobs and production from Canada to the United States. In general, neoclassical economists assumed that geography would have little influence over the effects of free trade. Opponents to free trade, on the other hand, made geographic assumptions to argue that continental market forces unleashed by free trade would have regionally diverse effects on North America, with Canada bearing more of the burden than the United States (Drache 1988). Opponents saw free trade between Canada and the United States as restricting the scope of political exchange in Canada, ultimately limiting Canadian sovereignty (Young 1989). They predicted that the FTA would diminish Canada's ability to address problems associated with Canada's vast land area and geographical diversity. Regional development programs and subsidies destined for Canada's hinterland regions could be targeted as unfair under free trade. They also predicted that without these programs, regional disparity and regional antagonisms would increase as the FTA hindered the implementation of nation-building policies.

A related argument points to the directional bias of market forces under free trade versus the directional bias that forms the basis of the Canadian nation. Canada was built on an east-west axis by a state that consciously imposed tariffs and underwrote the construction of a transcontinental railway to connect British Columbia to eastern Canada. The FTA and its implied deregulation was predicted to enhance the north-south (cross-border) axis at the expense of the historic east-west axis that formed the backbone of the Canadian nation. A nation-state such as Canada could expect profound restructuring when it becomes part of a continental market.

The most vocal Canadian opposition came from organized labor. Union leaders recognized that the FTA would increase capital mobility, thereby making individual Canadian unions and their communities increasingly susceptible to corporate threats of relocation. Organized labor opposed the FTA because they understood that Canadian unions were much stronger than their American counterparts (Davis 1986). Because the American economy is larger than the Canadian economy, Canadian workers would feel the strongest effects. The anticipated result of the harmonization was a downward spiral of wages and workers' rights in Canada to match those in the United States (O'Hagan 1986).

Increased capital mobility brings with it the threat of plant closures and job losses. Labor leaders predicted that management would force Canadian workers to make concessions when it threatened to relocate production to the United States. Because labor felt pressure to comply with corporate wage and work-rules demands, union leaders predicted that if jobs were to leave Canada, they would depart for those regions in the United States where unions were poorly organized and wages were lower than in Canada. They predicted that firms leaving Canada would avoid the strong union states of the American Midwest and relocate to those states where unions were weak or non-existent, for example in the South.

Consequences of Free Trade Six Years Later

Free trade proponents predicted significant improvements in job quantity and quality for North Americans under the stimulus of free trade. Opponents, on the other hand, predicted that the FTA would result in a loss of manufacturing jobs for Canada. Which side's predictions have proven more accurate?

By the end of 1994, it is clear that trade volume had increased between Canada and the United States. What FTA proponents failed to predict was the loss and out-migration of manufacturing jobs from Canada to the United States (Tables 11.1 and 11.2). Although trade has increased, jobs related to trade have not. A recession effect occurred in both countries but unemployment rates increased to a much greater extent in Canada than in the United States.

Table 11. 1: The Canadian Job Creation Potential of the FTA

Economic Sector	Predicted Change (1988) Percent	Actual Change (1992) Percent
Chemicals	-0.1	- 4.5
Clothing	+0.7	-25.0
Electrical Products	-1.4	-14.9
Food and Beverage	+0.8	- 4.0
Furniture and Fixtures	+0.4	-30.8
Machinery	+0.3	-22.6
Metal Fabrications	+0.4	-25.5
Motor Vehicles / Parts	+0.1	-11.5
Non-metallic Minerals	+0.4	-21.3
Petroleum and Coal	+0.3	-12.5
Primary Metals	+1.2	-17.8
Printing and Publishing	+2.4	- 8.5
Pulp and Paper	+0.2	-12.5
Rubber and Plastics	-0.7	- 8.9
Textiles	-0.8	-22.0
Wood Industries	+0.4	-16.5

Sources: Calculated from ECC 1988; *Statistics Canada 1992; Statistics Canada, 1995.*

Table 11. 2: Persons Employed in the Canadian Economy (thousands)

Year	Total	Manufacturing	Trade
1985	11,311	1,981	2,001
1987	11,861	2,018	2,097
1989	12,486	2,126	2,186
1991	12,340	1,865	2,169
1993	12,358	1,806	2,105

Source: *Statistics Canada* 1986, 1990, 1992b, 1993a

Finally, many firms and jobs relocated from Canada to the United States. Production costs were so low in other parts of North America that some companies closed their doors in Canada and moved south. Firms have shifted production and jobs from Canada to three areas of the United States: to American border states, to right-to-work states in the American Southeast, and to states in the industrial Midwest (Table 11.3). Firms that relocated to states along the Canadian-American border tended to be small, independent Canadian-owned companies with an average of only 36 jobs. The most often cited reason for moving production to this region was to take advantage of lower production costs in the United States while remaining close to the Canadian market (Wickens 1991; Chisholm 1991a and 1991b; Farnsworth 1991; Canadian Press 1992). The border states attracted the most firms but the fewest jobs of the three regions. This reflects the small scale and local focus of these predominantly Canadian-owned firms that had grown tired of high Canadian wages, taxes, and regulatory compliance costs.

Table 11.3: Job and Firm Relocation by Region, 1989 to 1994

Region	Jobs Shifted	Firms Shifted	Ratio
Border States	4,359	122	36
Right-to-work States	5,336	32	167
Industrial Heartland	12,844	62	207
United States Total	22,539	216	104

Source: Adapted from data in Merrett (1996)

American state and local agencies have spent millions of dollars in recruiting such firms since 1989. In the state of Washington, the Fourth Corner Economic Development Group has attracted investment to Bellingham (a city only fifty miles south of Vancouver) and surrounding Whatcom County using a combination of private and public development funds. When this local agency started in 1990, seventeen Canadian companies operated in Whatcom County. By 1993, that figure had risen to 100 Canadian firms employing 1,600 workers (Dalglish 1993). Tariff elimination under the FTA has permitted firms to shift production to Whatcom County where they can serve the Canadian market while enjoying the lower-wage, lower-tax environment of the United States. Similarly, efforts of the Buffalo Enterprise Development Corporation have resulted in the relocation of 91 Canadian firms to the Buffalo area (Dowling 1991; Canadian Press 1992).

Recruiting has played an important role in the movement of production from Canada to the right-to-work states as well. Officials from North Carolina visited 27 Canadian firms in 1992 to lure them south with promises of subsidized worker retraining, weak unions, low taxes, and low wages. Trade representatives say that Canada's pro-union stance and high wages are forcing companies south (Marotte 1992). In 1990, the average Canadian wage was C$16.02 per hour. The average U.S. wage was C$14.77 per hour whereas the average wage in North Carolina was only C$12.00 per hour (Marotte 1992). Firms shifting production from Canada to North Carolina can thereby save 25 percent on labor costs alone.

Although the right-to-work states had the lowest wages in the United States, they did not attract the most investment from Canada. Unexpectedly, the largest amount of Canadian investment was attracted to the American Midwest. Neither neoclassical economists or political economists anticipated that the Midwest would be such a popular corporate destination. Neoclassical economists believed that firm relocation would be negligible while the political economists believed that low-wage regions would benefit most at the expense of Canada. In fact, more jobs have been shifted from Canada to the industrial heartland than to any other region in the United States. Again, aggressive recruiting by state and local officials has played an important role. State development agencies from Illinois, Michigan, Ohio, and the Council of Great Lakes Governors established recruiting offices in Toronto.

The industrial heartland has attracted very large firms on average when compared to firms that shifted to border states. A large proportion of these firms are branch plants of large American multinational corporations that relocated to the United States to be close to the parent company (Gandhi 1993). The factories had been built in Canada to avoid the high tariffs at the Canadian border. Canada had a long history of using tariffs in its import-substitution development strategy. Free trade supporters said that these branch plants would remain in Canada after the implementation of the FTA and reconfigure their production to specialize as export platforms (Wonnacott and Hill 1987). In fact, the FTA had the opposite effect as it prompted the out-migration of dozens of branch plants from Canada to the United States. As tariffs dropped, multinational corporations moved production back to the United States where costs were lower than in Canada (Farnsworth 1991). The FTA (and now the North American Free Trade Agreement) makes it easier for firms to organize production, locate investment, source inputs, and determine prices according to continental rather than national development priorities (Campbell 1991). This explains why the Canadian subsidiaries of General Tire, B. F. Goodrich, and United Technologies moved back to the industrial heartland.

Canadian politicians adopted a trade policy based on neoclassical assumptions that eliminated jobs in Canada. When jobs are shifted out of a community, the negative consequences ripple through the local economy as fewer people spend money and the tax base shrinks. The direct job losses created by the shift of production also cause indirect job losses in the surrounding community. These effects can be estimated by using employment multipliers (Bluestone and Harrison 1982; Malecki 1991). It has been estimated that 22,539 Canadian jobs have been lost directly because of plant relocations to the United States. At the same time, indirect job losses because of plant relocations are estimated at 60,855 Canadian jobs. This figure does not include the estimated net loss of 350,000 manufacturing jobs in Canada that disappeared because of rationalization and merger processes linked to the FTA (Beauchesne 1992).

Overall, Canada has lost about 411,000 jobs because of restructuring and the relocation of production. The total number of Canadians employed in 1992 was estimated to be 12.2 million people (Statistics Canada 1993b). This means that the FTA eliminated 3.4 percent of the jobs in Canada. Canadian losses have far exceeded the worst-case scenario predicted by a University of Wisconsin study that concluded that Canada would lose at most 0.2 percent of its jobs (Schlefer 1992). In addition, many of the jobs that have vanished from Canada were high-wage jobs in the manufacturing sector.

Conclusions

The relocation of firms and jobs out of Canada undermines the assumptions made in neoclassical models that on first glance display "internal consistency and mathematical elegance "(Hufbauer and Schott 1992: 51). On second glance, we see that these assumptions were based on an array of faulty assumptions (Shaiken 1993). Neoclassical economists assumed that unemployment is a short-term effect of recessions. Canadian studies supporting free trade assumed full employment and a fixed volume of investment in both the United States and Canada. Under this assumption, capital would move to more productive sectors and regions within Canada but corporations would not widely shut down or move production to the United States (Schlefer 1992). The assumption of full employment was wrong because Canada had an unemployment rate of 8 percent in 1988 when most neoclassical studies were conducted. By 1993, the Canadian unemployment rate had risen to 11.4 percent (Statistics Canada 1992a, 1993b).

More importantly, economists supporting FTA failed to make the most important assumption of all: that geography matters. Economists ignored geography by assuming firms would not relocate outside of Canada under free trade (Wonnacott and Hill 1987). The ECC (1988, 27) said that "there is little evidence to support the idea that the agreement will lead to the 'de-industrialization' of Canada or to the exodus of manufacturing and other jobs from this country." The problem with this assertion is that evidence for job loss cannot be found if the possibility of job loss is not included as an assumption in the neoclassical model in the first place. The FTA created a continental market, yet economists modeled the effects of the FTA on a national basis. They ignored the implications for Canadian workers having to compete against workers in low-wage regions in the United States and now Mexico (CLC 1991). On the other hand, an economic model that acknowledged the importance of geography would assume that firms would exploit the differences in the variegated economic and political landscape of North America, not just Canada, in order to maximize profits. The political motivations of economic policy then become clear. Free trade agreements are part of broader strategy to benefit some firms and regions at the expense of others. Political geographers can take the example of free trade to show how the tension between nation-states and continental markets reveals the changing division and control of the earth's political and economic landscape.

Teaching the Political Geography of Free Trade

How can these considerations be conveyed to students in the classroom? One way students can learn about the effects of free trade is to engage them in a role-playing exercise that divides the class up into three (or more) groups. The first group represents Canadian unionized workers. The second group represents American factory owners. The third group represents Mexican peasant farmers. Each group is responsible for doing background research on the general political and economic geography of the country they are representing. Information they will require includes wage levels, occupational structure, and so on. World Bank Reports, the World Almanac, and United Nations documents containing such information are available in most school libraries.

In addition to the general background information, students in each group are asked to investigate whether their group supports or opposes free trade and why their group took that position. Newspapers, magazines, internet news groups and websites, and academic journals carry such information.

The general country information coupled with specific information about the region and population segment represented by each group allows for classroom discussion to take place. Each group must take a stand justifying why free trade is good or bad for their group specifically and why free trade is good or bad for North America generally. This role-playing can be expanded to include other groups such as Mexican bankers, Midwestern farmers, Canadian lumberjacks, or Mexican female factory workers. The purpose of this exercise is to get students to think about the different geographical regions, economic sectors, and population segments that are affected by public policy decisions such as free trade.

References

Beauchesne, E. 1992. "Crow Wants Inflation in Line with U.S. Rate," *Sault Star.* 17 January: A6.

Bluestone, Barry and Bennett Harrison 1982. *Deindustrialization of America.* New York: Basic Books.

Campbell, Bruce 1991. "Beggar Thy Neighbor," *The American Review of Canadian Studies.* 21 (2/3): 22-29.

Canadian Press 1988. "Unions May Scare Off U.S. Investment: Harvard," *Globe and Mail.* 1 December: B9.

_____ 1992. "Toronto Firm Decides on New York for Expansion," *Sault Star.* 29 February: A7.

_____ 1993. "Workers Stand Guard after Employer Pulls Out," *Sault Star.* 3 February: A1.

Canadian Labour Congress 1991. *Canadian Labour Congress Free Trade Briefing Document.* 7 (January): 1-82.

Chisholm, Patricia 1990. "The Flight of Industry: A High Cost Economy Takes the Rap," *Maclean's.* 3 December: 55.

_____ 1991a. "Giving Up, Moving Out: Canadian Manufacturers Say That Business is Better in the U.S," *Maclean's.* 18 March: 36-39.

_____ 1991b. "The Stampede to Buffalo," *Maclean's.* 18 March: 44.

Dalglish, Brenda. 1993. "Goin' Down the Road," *Maclean's.* 28 June: 28.

Davis, Mike. 1986. *Prisoners of the American Dream.* New York: Verso.

Dowling, Deborah 1991. "Shuffling off to Buffalo: Exodus Worries Business, Political Leaders," *Sault Star.* 26 October: A8.

Drache, Daniel 1988. "Canada in the American Empire," *Canadian Journal of Political and Social Theory.* 12 (1-2): 212-229.

Economic Council of Canada 1987. *Reaching Outward: A Statement by the Economic Council of Canada.* Ottawa: Ministry of Supply and Services.

_____ 1988. *Venturing Forth: An Assessment of the Canada-U.S. Trade Agreement, A Statement by the Economic Council of Canada.* Ottawa: Ministry of Supply and Services.

Farnsworth, Clyde. 1991. "Free-Trade Accord is Enticing Canadian Companies to the U.S.," *New York Times.* 9 August: A1, C3.

Gandhi, Prem 1991. "Trade and Investment Flows in New York State: Effects of the Free Trade Agreement." Pp. 89-100 in *Economic Opportunities in Freer U.S. Trade with Canada*, edited by Frederic Menz and Sarah Stevens. Albany: SUNY Press.

Geography for Life: National Geography Standards 1994. Washington, D.C.: National Geographic Research and Exploration for the American Geographical Society, Association of American Geographers, National Council for Geographic Education, and the National Geographic Society.

Gilpin, Robert 1987. *The Political Economy of International Relations.* Princeton, N.J.: Princeton University Press.

Harris, Richard and David Cox 1984. *Trade, Industrial Policy, and Canadian Manufacturing.* Toronto: Ontario Economic Council.

Harvey, David 1982 *The Limits to Capital.* Chicago: University of Chicago Press.

Hufbauer, Gary and Jeffrey J. Schott 1992. *North American Free Trade: Issues and Recommendations.* Washington, D.C.: Institute for International Economics.

Kidd, K. 1988. "Canadians Have an Eye on Buffalo for Business." *Toronto Star.* 19 November: C1.

Knox, P. and J. Agnew 1989. *The Geography of the World Economy.* London: Edward Arnold.

Krugman, Paul 1987. "Is Free Trade Passe?" *Economic Perspectives.* 1(2): 131-144.

Lipietz, Alain 1987. *Mirages and Miracles: The Crisis of Global Fordism.* New York: Verso.

Malecki, Edward 1991. *Technology and Economic Development: The Dynamics of Local, Regional, and National Change.* New York: Longmans.

Marotte, B. 1992. "North Carolina's Anti-Union Reputation Pays off." *Sault Star.* 1 August: A7.

Merrett, Christopher 1996. *Free Trade: Neither Free Nor about Trade.* Montreal: Black Rose Books.

O'Hagan, Dan 1986. "Free Trade, Our Canada or Theirs: Workers Confront the Corporate Blueprint." *Canadian Labour.* (September): 15-18.

Schlefer, J. 1992. "What Price Economic Growth?" *The Atlantic.* 270 (December): 114-118.

Shaiken, Harley. 1993. "Will Manufacturing Head South?" *Technology Review.* 24 (April): 28-29.

Statistics Canada. 1986. *Canadian Economic Observer.* Catalogue 11-010, January. Ottawa: Ministry of Supply and Services.

_____. 1990. *Canadian Economic Observer.* Catalogue 11-010, January. Ottawa: Ministry of Supply and Services.

_____. 1992a. *Canadian Social Trends.* Catalogue 11-008E. Number 24 (Summer). Ottawa: Ministry of Supply and Services.

_____. 1992b. *Canadian Economic Observer.* Catalogue 11-010, May. Ottawa: Ministry of Supply and Services.

_____. 1993a. *Canadian Economic Observer.* Catalogue 11-010, March. Ottawa: Ministry of Supply and Services.

_____. 1993b. *Canadian Economic Observer.* Catalogue 11-010, August. Ottawa: Ministry of Supply and Services.

_____. 1995. *Canadian Economic Observer.* Catalogue 11-010, April 1995. Ottawa: Ministry of Supply and Services.

Tremblay, Rodrigue. 1988. "250 Economists Say It's Our Best Option." Testimony to the House of Commons legislative committee on Bill C-130, a bill to enact the Canada-U.S. Free Trade Agreement, *Canadian Speeches.* 2. Ottawa, 26 July. (August/September): 5 6.

Trickey, Mike. 1991a. "Trade Offices Bring Message North: U.S. Open for Business." *Sault Star.* 29 June : A8.

Wickens, Barbara. 1991. "A Fresh Breath of Optimism." *Maclean's.* 18 March: 39.

Wonnacott, Paul and Roderick Hill. 1987. *Canadian and U.S. Adjustment Policies in a Bilateral Trade Agreement.* Washington, D.C.: Canadian-American Committee.

Young, R. A. 1989. "Political Scientists, Economists, and the Canada-U.S. Free Trade Agreement." *Canadian Public Policy.* 15 (1): 49-56.

CHAPTER 12
TEACHING GLOBAL ENVIRONMENTAL CHANGE AS LOCAL POLITICAL CONFLICT
William D. Solecki and Shira Birnbaum

Although debate about the speed, direction, and even the ultimate cause of global environmental change continues, the vast majority of natural scientists agree that the earth is experiencing a period of fundamental environmental change (Houghton *et al.* 1996; Kates *et al.* 1990). Scientific evidence increasingly indicates that human activity is playing a role in various ecological transformations. One of the most important scientific and policy concerns at the end of the twentieth century, global environmental change has been defined as two intersecting processes. One relates to global-scale processes such as global atmospheric and oceanic circulation. The second is associated with local-scale processes such as deforestation, land cover change, and biodiversity loss that are occurring in many places throughout the world (Meyer and Turner 1995; Adger and Brown 1994; Turner *et al.* 1990).

The prospect of global environmental change has important implications for agricultural production, public health, coastal development, and resource management (Stern *et al.* 1993; U.S. National Academy of Sciences 1991). It strikes at the heart of contemporary social issues such as hunger, malnutrition, equity, poverty, infectious disease, and sustainable development. As the earth's ecosystems change, questions have emerged regarding what society should do in response to these changes. Policy analysts, political scientists, geographers, as well as the news media and the general public are now examining the policy and political ramifications of global environmental change (Porter and Brown 1995; Johnston *et al.* 1995).

Much of the analysis so far has focused on global-scale geopolitical developments such as the emergence of international environmental agreements and the changing character of international trade. Although geopolitics is an important topic for analysis, we believe it does not fully address all the political geography questions associated with the topic of global environmental change. Instead, we suggest that we must examine global environmental change within the context of local small-scale political conflicts.

Our objective in this chapter is to demonstrate that improving our understanding of the human dimensions of global environmental change can occur only when viewed through the lens of political conflicts occurring within towns, counties, and states. In this chapter, we examine two broad categories of local political conflict associated with global environmental change. These include disputes about the nature and cause of global environmental change and the actions necessary to respond to these concerns.

Analysis of local political conflict should improve students' understanding of the root causes of global environmental change, as well as some of the impediments to effective societal response. A discussion of global environmental change within the context of local political conflict can also help reveal to students the importance of several underlying societal issues such as equity, the link between individual rights vs. community responsibility, and the connections between local places and global processes (Bruce *et al.* 1996; Kasperson 1994; Rees 1991). Students should not view global environmental change as something occurring on some abstract global scale detached from their everyday experience. Rather, we can encourage students to discover that fundamental shifts in the global environment occur locally through everyday political conflicts.

What follows here is a brief discussion of current scientific understanding of the process of global environmental change. Following this is an analysis of some ways in which political geographers analyze the societal aspects of global environmental change. This is followed by a discussion of two points of intersection between global environmental change and local political conflict. We also include an appendix of research and data sources useful for teachers discussing global environmental change. Numbers in brackets throughout the text identify references to specific resources in the Instructional Resources List at the end of the chapter.

The Process of Global Environmental Change

Global environmental change can be divided into three broad classes of physical phenomena: atmospheric change, oceanic change, and terrestrial change. The first two classes define large-scale changes in the composition and functioning of global atmospheric circulation patterns. Scientific evidence of changes in the atmosphere and world climate systems became widespread during the late 1970s. By the middle and late 1980s, the scientific and popular literature widely discussed and debated atmospheric and climate-change issues such as ozone depletion, acid rain, the greenhouse effect, and global warming.

Several underlying issues came to the fore in this period. Scientific understanding of regional and global-scale processes of atmospheric chemistry and circulation systems improved. Scientists recognized that the alteration of these systems might be having a deleterious effect on global ecological and human health [8, 10]. Although the precise causal links between increased levels of pollutants and global- and regional-scale atmospheric changes have been difficult to determine, the scientific literature throughout the 1980s offered increasing evidence of association among them. More sophisticated and complex models of global atmospheric processes made it possible to envision multiple, complex implications of global climate change. Scientists noted that positive and negative feedback loops could lead to secondary changes such as alterations in ocean circulation patterns, melting of the polar ice caps, and sea-level rise [5, 7]. Most global climate change models also predict increased variability in local weather regimes. This could result in higher maximum temperatures, longer droughts, and stronger storms in the future.

Atmospheric and oceanic changes may also be linked to terrestrial changes, or changes in the physical geography and ecology of the earth's land surface. Terrestrial changes associated with atmospheric and oceanic changes include changes in biodiversity and the range of species, and in rates of agricultural productivity (Watson *et al.* 1996). Evidence now indicates that land use and land cover shifts are occurring at a rapid rate throughout the world. Driven by the demands for agricultural production and natural resource extraction, changes in local practices result in increased deforestation, soil erosion, desertification, and declines in biodiversity.

Political Geography and Global Environmental Change

As sophistication of the natural science of global environmental change has increased, a set of social science questions also has emerged. Each of the social science disciplines has begun to address questions of global environmental change from its singular vantage point (Redclift 1995; Redclift and Benton 1994) [1, 2, 4, 6, 10, 11]. Political geography is no exception. Studies addressing the question of global environmental change are now exploring basic themes of research developed in Anglo-American political geography (see Shelley *et al* 1996 and Demko and Wood 1994 for recent reviews of political geography).

Most of the political geography analyses of the human dimensions of global environmental change have focused on international agreements and the geopolitics of global environmental policy-making. Examples include the Montreal Protocol on Ozone Depletion in 1989, the United Nations Environment Programme Biodiversity Treaty of 1992 as well as the actions of international study groups and conferences such as the International Panel on Climate Change (IPCC) and the United Nations Conference on the Environment and Development (see Porter and Brown 1995 and Johnston *et al.* 1995 for recent reviews).

Another thread of political geography research focused on global environmental change is based on political economy. Studies of this type focus on the societal processes that cause or aggravate environmental change and make certain populations vulnerable to its effects. A common focus of these studies is the character of nature-society interactions, including such things as, for example, the distribution of economic risk among farmers, the allocation of common property resources within socially stratified villages, or the effects of international timber trade policies on power relations within communities reliant upon timber harvesting.

Geographers have also examined the nature of societal response to global environmental change within the context of risk analysis and hazards management (Thornes 1995; Kasperson 1994; Riebsame 1990; Riebsame and Jacobs 1988). This research focuses on actions that might be undertaken in response to global environmental changes. Some studies examine how societies can make small-scale adjustments or large-scale adaptations to the ecological shifts brought on by global environmental change. These studies focus on how agricultural practices can be adjusted to accommodate increased annual temperatures, or how architecture and planning in coastal communities can respond to sea-level rise and the increased risk of powerful storms. Other policy studies focus on the issue of remediation, or how societies can act to lessen the likelihood of global environmental change. Analysts working in this vein might study ways that the rate of tropical deforestation could be slowed, or ways in which the volume of anthropogenic carbon dioxide releases could be reduced.

Understanding Global Environmental Change as Local Political Conflict

Although the causes and effects of large-scale environmental change may be global, response to such changes is often local. Within the local political arena many conflicts involving resource management, environmental pollution, response to natural hazards, and other environmental issues are articulated and resolved.

Local political conflicts occur in communities as individuals and interests vie for power and access to resources. Underpinning these conflicts often are difficult questions of value and equity. Within any community, distinct groups might have differing perceptions of the value and usefulness of key resources. Conflict often centers around debates over which group's definitions and values will prevail in decision-making processes, and over the relative distribution of the benefits and costs of decision-making. Many such analyses are based on the general objective that the greatest number of benefits should accrue to the most people. This goal, however, becomes complicated and often elusive as deep-seated problems emerge regarding matters of class, race, gender, location, age, or, explicitly in the case of global environmental change, scientific uncertainty. Environmental conflicts at the local level are imbued to the core with these complex issues of societal equity.

The character of local political conflicts has been examined in many settings, including those involving the siting of locally-unwanted land uses (LULUs) and those experiencing the development and implementation of new public policies (see Agnew 1987). Our intent here is to point to how they illustrate fundamental issues of political geography that can be accessible to students. The discussion below offers two examples of how global environmental change is associated with and expressed through local political conflict. The first example focuses on how environmental change takes place and how the power structures of local communities debate the responses. The second focuses on the politics of policy development and implementation. Both examples illustrate the degree to which an analysis of local political conflict can point to key issues for discussion in the environmental classroom. Local disputes, as will be seen, can offer good illustrations of the nuanced complexity of global environmental change. Analyzing these disputes can help students grasp the everyday, almost mundane, nature of serious global problems and the way they play out in terms of local struggles for money, power, or both.

The Cause of Environmental Change as Political Conflict

Where environmental change is taking place, major disagreements over the definition of resources, over how people manage their resources, and how they should manage them in the future (Redclift and Benton 1994). The story of the Lwangwa National Park in Zambia (Blaikie 1995; Abel and Blaikie 1986) is a case in point. The Lwangwa Valley, located just northeast of the Zambian capital, Lusaka, has been home since before the turn of the century to a diverse array of groups of people. Each group uses the region's resources and defines their importance in a distinct way.

Among the groups active in recent years have been subsistence hunters who rely on the valley's resources for their basic survival; tourists and safari firms, who *sell* the region to an elite international market as a vacation experience; conservationists and scientists who worry about local ecosystem fragility; politicians and local and regional administrators who must respond to the wide-reaching efforts of changes in local and national conditions of poverty, population growth, urbanization, and labor markets; and poachers, whose activities are responsive to an illegal international market for the elephant ivory and rhinoceros horns that they harvest in the valley.

Reports of ecological change, including loss of certain plant and animal species and suppression of long-standing patterns of species diversity, date back many decades and became increasingly widespread starting in the 1940s. Some of these changes, according to scientific evidence, could be traced to changes in patterns of global resource use as influenced by wider social and economic trends. The development of a rural road system in Zambia enabled increased human access to the region, for example, while increasing regional poverty and associated labor market changes fostered intensified local resource extraction.

Increasing international demand for ivory combined with changes in the availability of firearms also contributed to ecological changes. The valley ecosystem was based on a complex web of interconnections in which the size and range of certain animal populations affected the size and range of the population of plants on which they grazed. Sanctuaries were established in the valley in 1902 and 1940. Zambian national park policy, following international conventions, was aimed at ecosystem preservation and tourism promotion. Right from the outset, interestingly, the very definition of a *natural area*—a place ostensibly free of human intervention and worthy of preservation in a pristine state—was laden with political overtones favoring some local interests over others.

By the 1980s, as ecological changes intensified, the combination of natural and societal processes had made the region a site of considerable local conflict, and expert managers were brought in to develop a management plan that could cause compromise among the conflicting groups and achieve a durable political truce in the valley. Taking what seemed like a reasonable, rational approach, the plan appealed to the ability of the different actors and interest groups to negotiate a mutually beneficial resolution. Not surprisingly, this has been an elusive goal, and political conflicts continue to be played out among the various actors. Differing levels of access to political authority and social status among interest groups continue to result in differing levels of ability to achieve political goals. Social relations may be defined in environmental terms, and environmental relations are mediated in the realm of social life.

From the start, competing claims on resources aggravated, if not triggered, ecological transformations in the park. Then, subsequent political responses were themselves worked out through social stratifications in the community. Pre-existing political alliances and allegiances based on culture, class, and economic interests created barriers for certain policy initiatives just as they created opportunities for others. Neither the ecological transformation nor the responses to them were matters purely of science and objective technical expertise. For students, the case highlights this key theme of political geography.

Global Environmental Change Public Policy as Political Conflict

A second example demonstrates how we can associate global environmental change with and express it in local political conflict by examining the policy response to stratospheric ozone in the United States. In the mid 1970s, scientific evidence emerged linking global ozone depletion with the use of chlorofluorocarbons (CFCs) in air conditioning and refrigeration units, aerosol cans, and in cleaners for computer circuit boards. Ozone depletion resulting in increased ultraviolet radiation had been associated with increases in the likelihood of skin cancer, cataracts, and immune disorders. The discovery led legislators in the U.S. in 1978 to ban the use of chlorofluorocarbons in aerosol cans.

In 1985, a British scientist detected a large and growing hole in the ozone layer above Antarctica. This widely publicized discovery prompted the writing of the Montreal Protocol on substances that deplete the ozone layer, a major international agreement signed by more than 120 nations in 1987. The agreement called for a 50 percent reduction in the use and manufacture of CFCs in the U.S. and other developed nations by the year 2000, with developing nations to comply by 2015.

Further scientific research fueled further policy development, and in 1989 Congress passed a tax on CFCs as an incentive to U.S. firms to reduce production and develop less harmful alternatives. Amendments to the federal Clean Air Act in 1990 granted the President authority to phase out CFC production before the internationally agreed deadline if new scientific evidence seemed to warrant it. The evidence came in 1992, when NASA studies were released documenting high levels of chlorine over New England, Canada, and Europe. Around the nation, municipal governments and state legislatures passed local laws aimed at reducing CFC emissions, including laws banning the release of CFCs by air-conditioning and auto-repair firms. In response, President George Bush announced that he would move up to 1995 the deadline for a U.S. phase-out of CFC production. Ozone became part of popular consciousness as sun-screen manufacturers responded to media reports by adding ultraviolet protection to advertising for their product lines. In 1995, a Nobel Prize in chemistry was awarded to the scientist who had first linked CFCs to ozone depletion. CFC regulation turned out to be a complicated affair governed less by purely scientific evidence than by the nuances of politics and the marketplace.

Many firms had developed or were using alternatives to CFC. One IBM plant in California, made a highly publicized switch to plain soap and water for cleaning computer circuit boards. Throughout the early 1990s the price of CFCs had soared to more than 10 times the pre-regulation price per pound. One reason was that auto- and air-conditioning repair firms were stockpiling CFCs grandfathered in by loopholes in the regulations. Consumers started feeling the effects of high prices. Those with old cars or old air conditioning units could pay either top dollar for stockpiled CFCs or could pay to have their air conditioners retro-fitted for compatibility with the emerging class of CFC alternatives.

By late 1995, as some business and consumer groups complained about increasing costs, it became evident that a thriving black market had developed for illegal CFC shipments. In international trade centers in Florida and California, representatives of the Central Intelligence Agency, Customs Service, Environmental Protection Agency, and Federal Bureau of Investigation had joined several international law enforcement agencies in intercepting multi-million dollar shipments of illegal CFCs, coming mostly from producers in Mexico, Russia, and India. Operation Cool Breeze launched a new federal effort to stop the illegal trade in what law enforcement officers were calling Miami Ice.

Meanwhile, on the political front, business people attempted to roll back what they perceived was an environmental extremist federal invasion of local and state's rights. In mid 1995, the Arizona legislature passed a law allowing CFCs to be manufactured and used in Arizona. The law was more of a self-conscious public statement than a substantive change in actual policies, since states cannot declare themselves exempt from federal regulation. Still, highly publicized debates over the matter reflected the degree to which environmental policy debates boil in the crucible of complex pre-existing political and ideological conflicts. Ironically, U.S. chemical manufacturers produced nearly 75 percent as much CFC in 1995 as they had produced in 1993, using legal exemptions allowing production for export to developing nations. The development and implementation of an international environmental policy were mediated at the local level by the politics of trade and long standing debates regarding the relative power of state and federal lawmakers.

Conclusion

By situating global ecological transformations in their local contexts, teachers can help students discover the socio-political processes at work in environmental conditions and in policy development and implementation. We chose two case studies to illustrate some of these possibilities, but teachers will certainly find that illustrations abound in their own communities. A discussion of global environmental change as local political conflict can get students thinking critically about connections between the political and the ecological. Just as importantly, it will encourage them to discover their position in earth history and imagine the possibility of their participation in shaping a world in which they would want to live.

References Cited

Abel, N., and P. Blaikie. 1986. "Elephants, People, Parks, and Development: The Case of the Lwangwa Valley, Zambia," *Environmental Management*, 10: 735-751.

Adger, W. N., and K. Brown. 1994. *Land Use and the Causes of Global Warming*. New York: John Wiley & Sons.

Agnew, J. 1987. *Place and Politics: The Geographical Mediation of State and Society*. Boston: Allen & Unwin.

Blaikie, P. 1995. "Changing Environments or Changing Views?" *Geography*, 80: 203-214.

Bruce, J. L. H., and E. Haits eds. 1996. Climate Change 1995: *Economic and Social Dimensions of Climate Change*. New York: Cambridge University Press.

Demko, G. J., and W. B. Wood, eds. 1994. *Reordering the World: Geopolitical Perspectives on the Twenty-first Century*. Boulder, Colo.: Westview.

Houghton, J. T., M. L. G. Filho, B. A. Callander, N. Harris, A. Kattenberg, and K. Maskell eds. 1996. *Climate Change 1995: The Science of Climate Change*. New York: Cambridge University Press.

Johnston, R. J., P. J. Taylor, and M. J. Watts eds. 1995. *Geographies of Global Change: Remapping the World in the Late Twentieth Century*. Cambridge, Mass.: Blackwell.

Kasperson, R. 1994. "Global Environmental Hazards: Political Issues in Societal Responses." Pp. 141-166 in *Reordering the World: Geopolitical Perspectives on the Twenty-first Century*, edited by G. J. Demko and W. B. Wood. Boulder, Colo.: Westview Press.

Kates, R. W., B. L. Turner II, W. C. Clark, J. F. Richards, J. T. Mathews, and W. B. Meyer eds. 1990. *The Earth as Transformed by Human Action*. New York: Cambridge University Press.

Meyer, W. B. and B. L. Turner. 1995. "The Earth Transformed: Trends, Trajectories, and Patterns," Pp. 302-317 in *Geographies of Global Change: Remapping the World in the Late Twentieth Century*, edited by R. J. Johnston, P. J. Taylor, and M. J. Watts. Cambridge, Mass: Blackwell.

National Academy of Sciences 1991. *Policy Implications of Greenhouse Warming*. Washington, D.C.: National Academy Press.

Porter, G. and Brown, J. 1995. *Global Environmental Politics*. Boulder, Colo.: Westview Press.

Redclift, M. R. 1995. "Global Environmental Change: The Contribution of Social Science Research to Policy in The U.K.," *The Environmentalist*. 15: 240-245.

Redclift, M. R., and T. Benton eds. 1994. *Social Theory and the Global Environment*. London: Routledge.

Rees, J. 1991. "Equity and Environmental Policy," *Geography* 76: 292-303.

Riebsame, W. E. 1990. "Anthropogenic Climate Change and a New Paradigm of Natural Responses Planning," *Professional Geographer.* 42: 1-12.

Riebsame, W. E., and Jacobs, J. W. 1988. "Climate Change and Water Resources in the Sacramento-San Joaquin Region of California." Boulder: Institute of Behavioral Science, University of Colorado, Working Paper #64.

Shelley, F. M., J. C. Archer, F. M. Davidson, and S. D. Brunn. 1996. *Political Geography of the United States.* New York: Guilford Press.

Stern, P. C. *et al.* eds. 1993. *Global Environmental Change: The Human Dimensions.* Washington, D.C.: National Academy Press.

Thornes, J. 1995. "Global Environmental Change and Regional Response: The European Mediterranean," *Transactions of the Institute of British Geographers,* 20: 357-367.

Watson, R. T., M. C. Zinyowera, and R. H. Moss eds. 1996. Climate Change 1995: Impacts, *Adaptations and Mitigation: Scientific-Technical Analyses.* New York: Cambridge University Press.

Instructional Resources for the Human Dimensions of Global Environmental Change

Agencies/Organizations/Work Groups
1. Consortium for International Earth Science Information Network CIESIN. WWW site: http://www.ciesin.org

2. Global Change Specialty Group of the Association of American Geographers. WWW site: http://www.geog.utah.edu/~hdgcsg/index.html

3. International Geosphere Biosphere Programme: A Study of Global Change. An interdisciplinary scientific activity established and sponsored by the International Council of Scientific Unions ICSU. WWW site: http://www.igbp.kva.se/

4. International Human Dimensions of Global Change Programme IHDP. Formerly known as the Human Dimensions of Global Environmental Change Programme. Co-sponsored by the International Social Science Council and the International Council of Scientific Unions. WWW site: http://www.ciesin.org/TG/HDP/hdp.html

5. Intergovernmental Panel on Climate Change IPCC. Established by the United Nations Environment Programme and World Meteorological Organization in 1988, to assess scientific information about climate change relevant for international and national policy formulation. WWW site: http://www.usgrp.gov/ipcc/

6. Second Commission on College Geography CCG2 project on Developing Active Learning Modules on the Human Dimensions of Global Change. Five modules have been developed and focus on the following topics: 1. Overview and Introduction to the Human Dimensions of Global Change; 2. Health Effects of Global Climate Change; 3. Risk/Hazards and Global Change; 4. Urbanization and Global Environmental Change; 5. Technological Change/Industrial Metabolism. Contact person: Dr. Susan Hanson, School of Geography, Clark University, Worcester, MA 01610. Internet: ccg2@clarku.edu.

7. U.S. Global Change Research Information Office. Provides access to global change and environmental data and information from around the world. WWW Site: http://www.gcrio.org/edu.html

8. U.S. Global Change Research Program. WWW Site: http://www.usgcrp.gov Journals/Other Regular Publications/World Web Sites

9. *Ambio: Journal of the Human Environment.* A journal published by the Royal Swedish Academy of Sciences.

10. *Consequences: The Nature & Implications of Environmental Change.* A journal published by the Saginaw Valley State University with funding provided by the U.S. National Oceanic and Atmospheric Administration, National Aeronautic Space Administration, and National Science Foundation.

11. *Global Environmental Change: Human and Policy Dimensions.* A journal published by Butterworth-Heineman in cooperation with United Nations University.

12. Global Environmental Policy Research Tools-Marc Levy/Princeton. WWW site: http://www.princeton.edu/~mlevy/

13. *Human Dimensions Quarterly.* A journal published by the Consortium for International Earth Science Information Network CIESIN

14. Global Change Master Directory. WWW site: http://gcmd.gsfc.nasa.gov/

15. Planet Earth Home Page. WWW site: http://www.nosc.mil/planet_earth/weather.html 16. U.S. National Science Foundation Global Change Research. WWW site: http://www.nsf.gov/stratare/egch/start.htm

CHAPTER 13
THE DYNAMIC POLITICAL MAP
Alice T. M. Rechlin Perkins

The forces of cooperation and conflict among the peoples of the world, as addressed in National Geography Standard 13, *Geography for Life* (1994), play a major role in determining the boundaries of political and social regions on Earth. Boundaries of social regions usually represent broad transitional zones. Political boundaries, however, represent abrupt transitions separating territory under the sovereignty of one state from that of another. Distinct boundaries on the world's political map reflect the state of cooperation and conflict among Earth's peoples at that point in history represented by the map.

Boundary lines, together with the names of places and other geographic features, provide a visual image of human control over the lands and seas of the planet. As humans continue to vie with each other over territories and resources, the lines on the political map will continue to change. Frequently, place-name changes accompany alterations in boundaries. Boundary and place-name changes may be rapid, reflecting upheaval and political instability, or they may be gradual, signifying a deliberate, negotiated, territorial transfer of ownership and power.

The issue of boundary changes is considered in several of the other essays in this volume. The purpose of this chapter is to address the kinds of issues and questions geographers and cartographers must confront when keeping track of these changes. All of issues are related to questions of control resulting from conflict and cooperation.

At the entrance to the Cartographic Division in the National Geographic Society in Washington, D.C., is a plaque inscribed with a quotation from Gilbert Hovey Grosvenor, the *National Geographic's* first editor. Grosvenor stated that "A map is the greatest of all epic poems. Its lines and colors show the realization of great dreams." At first glance these words seem to convey a sense of valiancy, boldness, and heroism. Upon further reflection, however, these words are wrought with a more ominous meaning. One might rightfully ponder whose "realized dreams" are depicted by the lines and names on the map, and at what cost to human life and suffering.

For example, boundaries in the Balkans of southeastern Europe are currently disputed. Some dream of keeping the republic of Bosnia and Herzegovina intact, and others dream of a greater Serbia. Should the dreams of a greater Serbia prevail, one might wonder what this will mean for the Bosnian Muslims. Will Bosnia and Herzegovina continue to exist as a separate political entity? How will the Croatians fare in this struggle for territorial control and power? It is this human propensity to control space, from personal space to national and supranational space that plays the major role in determining the political map of the world. Keep in mind that shifts in boundary alignments on a map frequently follow the death and suffering of thousands of people.

Recent Changes to the World Political Map
Several major boundary changes to the world political map have occurred since 1990. In November of 1989 the Berlin Wall between East and West Germany fell. Less than a year later, the two Germanys achieved unification, which erased the boundary between them. A few months later the Soviet Union began to disintegrate. In less than a year, one country became fifteen separate political states. In 1992, Yugoslavia broke into five independent countries. On January 1, 1993, Czechoslovakia became the Czech Republic and Slovakia. Later that year, Walvis Bay reverted to Namibia, and Eritrea broke from Ethiopia to became a sovereign state. The year 1994 saw the birth of independent Palau (an archipelago in the western Pacific Ocean about 500 miles southeast of the Philippines) along with the abolition of homelands within South Africa. Today we may be witnessing the birth of a new country in the Gaza strip and the West Bank, both of which were occupied by Israel after the Six Day War in 1967.

People are highly sensitive to maps depicting boundaries, particularly those that portray new boundary configurations. For instance, in May 1994 problems arose at the ceremonial signing of the peace accord between Israel and Palestine. The Israeli Prime Minister, Yitzhak Rabin, and the leader of the Palestine Liberation Organization, Yasser Arafat, were willing to sign the accord, but Arafat refused to sign the accompanying maps that would delimit the areal extent of PLO authority. After several tense moments and additional negotiations, Arafat agreed to sign but he appended a notation that the maps were approved subject to modification. Rabin is reported to have said, "We had a dream before we had a map. Now, we have a map and a dream together."

Alterations in map colors, line positions, and place names are manifestations of political and territorial changes on Earth's surface. These changes will continue as the diverse peoples of Earth address the hundreds of contested borders scattered around the world. Any one of these problem borders can spark an emotionally charged incident leading to political upheaval and bloodshed.

An example of the volatile nature of boundary problems can be found in the flare-up between Ecuador and Peru in 1995 over their long-standing border disagreement (Figure 13.1).

Figure 13.1 Ecuador and Peru Border Disputes

The seeds of that dispute were sown when the Spanish crown divided the land almost a century and a half ago. Tensions over the border erupted in war between Ecuador and Peru in 1941. Other countries in the Americas, including the United States, put pressure upon the two countries to sign the Protocol of Rio de Janeiro to end the conflict. The United States put pressure on the two countries to sign the Protocol to present a unified hemispheric front against the Axis powers in World War II. This protocol, however, reduced Ecuador to half its previous size. Now that the border section is reputed to contain rich deposits of gold and uranium, the territorial dispute has surfaced once again. Four countries, Argentina, Brazil, Chile, and the United States, are currently attempting to broker a permanent peace.

Place-Name Changes

Major political changes frequently carry significant place-name changes. It is not uncommon to use names as rewards or punishments. This has been evident in Russia during and after the period of Communist rule. After the Russian Revolution, Saint Petersburg became Leningrad. Three-quarters of a century later, after the dissolution of the Soviet Union, the city's name was changed back to Saint Petersburg. Similarly, the city of Volgograd had been named Stalingrad but the name reverted to Volgograd after Stalin fell out of favor.

Further, when the newly independent republics of the former Soviet Union gained their independence they were eager to return to their former languages and alphabets. For the cartographer publishing in a language with a different alphabet, this requires that all place names be transliterated from the reestablished alphabet, and then translated into the publisher's language. This is a time-consuming process requiring linguistic experts who have the ability to romanize place name spellings from other alphabets.

An example of the magnitude of the problem for the map maker can be seen in Figure 13.2 illus-

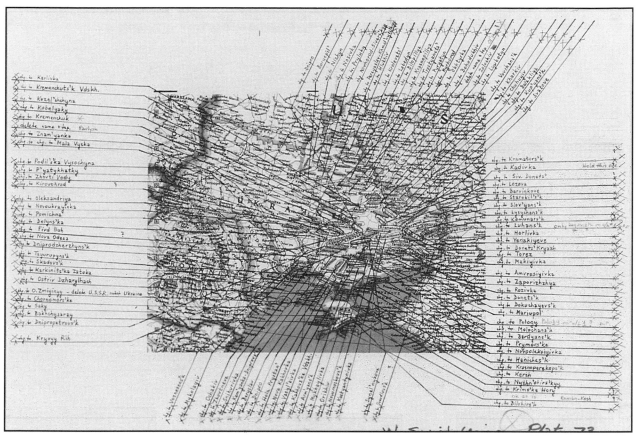

Figure 13.2. Map of Ukraine with Name Changes (courtesy *National Geographic* 1993)

trating the number of name changes called for immediately after Ukraine changed from the Russian cyrillic to Ukrainian cyrillic. Currently Ukraine is refining its transliteration system. Once completed, new spellings for the English versions of the place names, and, of course, new maps, will be required.

Keeping up with the Changes

During the summer of 1995, the National Geographic Cartographic Division's staff was hard at work revising the *National Geographic Atlas of the World.* All map plates were to be completed and ready for the presses by August of that year. In June a rumor that the English spelling of "Kazakstan" was to be changed from "Kazakhstan" reached the Division's staff. A new spelling must be verified prior to calling for a change on the map. Sources at the United Nations confirmed the rumor with a copy of a letter from the Ambassador of the Republic of Kazakstan to the Secretary General of the United Nations. On June 19, the United States Board on Geographic Names recommended the new spelling be adopted. The former spelling, "Kazahkstan" with an "h," was a result of transliteration from the Russian cyrillic. The new spelling, minus the "h," maintains the Kazak phonetic sound in the English pronunciation.

Changing the spelling of even one country name is more difficult than one might think. For example, the change from "Kazakhstan" to "Kazakstan" required no less than 21 map or text plates on which the old name "Kazakhstan" appeared to be changed. By mid-June most of the maps had already passed the preliminary proofreading stage. Some had even gone through final proofreading. Every plate that might possibly carry the name in question had to be scrutinized once again to be sure that the changes were made.

Other changes in place names are more controversial. An example is F.Y.R.O.M. One might ask, "What is F.Y.R.O.M.?, Where is F.Y.R.O.M.? Who ever heard of F.Y.R.O.M.?"

F.Y.R.O.M. stands for "The Former Yugoslav Republic of Macedonia." When Yugoslavia disintegrated and the province of Macedonia became a sovereign state, much dissension arose over the use of "Macedonia" as the name of this newly independent country. The northern section of Greece forms the southern extension of the region known as Macedonia. Visions of aggression to expand the territory of the new country to encompass this area of Greece alarmed some Greek officials. To add further to their consternation, Macedonia's new flag contained the Vergina Sun. The Vergina Sun was the historic emblem of Philip of Macedon, father of Alexander the Great. Greece claimed the sole right to use the Vergina Sun. So outraged was Greece over what it saw as usurpation of its name and symbol that it did not lift its trade embargo with Macedonia until Macedonia dropped the symbol in February, 1994.

The name remains an issue between Greece and Macedonia. In order to gain membership in the United Nations the name Macedonia could not be used alone. In order to be granted United Nations membership, the new country agreed to be referred to as "The Former Yugoslav Republic of Macedonia." When the United States recognized Macedonia's sovereignty it did so by capitalizing the first letter of each of the words making up its name. Therefore, in the United States the "f" in "former" is also capitalized, which is not the case in the United Nations. The capitalization affects the seating in the General Assembly, which is undertaken in alphabetical order in English. Had the "t" been lower cased, the Macedonian delegation would be seated between Finland and France, rather than between Thailand and Togo. Protocol for the Olympic Games, in which national teams enter the Olympic stadium in alphabetical order, would similarly be affected.

Greece is adamant that the full name of the new country be used, even on maps. However, the long name can usually not be fitted into the space outlining the country except on very large-scale maps. This leaves the map maker with the alternative of using the letters "F.Y.R.O.M." Should that, too, be impossible, the space on the maps might be identified by the acronym, FYROM. Should that happen people will know it by its initials risking the possibility of eventually losing sight of its Macedonian roots. How long will it be before the world begins to call the country by its acronym?

Place-Name Information Sources

The United Nation's Translations Division and Cartographic Section of the Department of Economics and Social Development is a valuable sources of place-name information. In fact the Translations Division publishes a Terminology Bulletin entitled *Country Names*. This gives the official name of each member country of the U.N. with the official spellings in the six official languages of the United Nations (English, French, Spanish, Russian, Chinese, and Arabic).

The United Nations also involves itself with the standardization of place names through its Group of Experts on Geographic Names. Representatives from different countries are seated on this committee according to language groupings. They meet every two years in either New York or Geneva. The group grapples with transliteration systems and name standardization policies. Its members also sponsor training workshops in countries that are just beginning to address the issue of name standardization.

A second excellent source of information dealing with country names and capital cities is the U.S. Department of State in Washington, D.C. The State Department list of countries and their capitals is available on the Internet.

One of the most important sources for official place names and their spellings in this country is the United States Board on Geographic Names. The Board was created by President Benjamin Harrison in 1890, at a time characterized by confusion caused by the use of different names for the same river, mountain, town, or other geographic feature. Some of the names appearing on the survey maps were new. Others turned out to be new names for settlements that had already been named. Still others were new translations from Spanish or French names. As a result considerable confusion over the location of places stemmed from the naming and renaming of geographic features by several people who had explored, surveyed, or settled the area independently. The Board was empowered to resolve these controversies and standardize the names.

Today, the Board on Geographic Names has two separate committees, the Foreign Names Committee and the Domestic Names Committee. Representatives from several government agencies with an interest in the standardization of geographic names sit on these committees. The work of the Foreign Names Committee is supported by linguists and language experts employed at the Defense Mapping Agency. This team studies new map sources from all over the world to ascertain name changes and transliteration issues. The recent independence of the former republics of the Soviet Union engendered a flurry of activity as cartographers all over the country looked for guidance in updating their maps. This same team is responsible for the research information that goes into the gazetteer updates of the world's 192 independent countries. Today the public can access the foreign names database through the World Wide Web.

The Domestic Names Committee meets monthly to deliberate policy matters and to make decisions regarding the naming and spelling of specific places or features that are brought to its attention either by individuals or by State Boards on Geographic Names. The Domestic Names Committee have declared the words "Nigger" and "Jap" pejorative and therefore are not admissible for naming places or geographic features in this country. These pejorative terms were removed from the federal maps as new printings of the maps were made.

Other proposed names and name changes are considered by the committee on a case-by-case basis. However, some Native American tribes have been objecting to the use of the word "squaw" on maps. This is particularly true of tribal groups in Minnesota and Arizona. In fact, the State Board on Geographic Names in Minnesota has decreed that all place names that include the word "squaw" must be changed. If all tribal groups in the country were to consider "squaw" to be a pejorative term, and if the federal government were to declare "squaw" a derogatory term, more than 1200 geographic place names and features in this country would have to be renamed. Among these would be the well-known resort of Squaw Valley, California, which was the site of the Winter Olympic Games in 1960.

Some Interesting Observations

People try to name, or rename, places and features regularly. Recently there was an attempt to rename Mobile Bay, Alabama. A member of a Pentecostal church near Mobile, Alabama was on a church dinner-cruise one evening when he became inspired to try to change the name of the bay on which he was floating. In late 1994 the *Mobile Register* reported that the proponent of the name change related that God wanted him to restore the bay's former name, the "Bay of the Holy Spirit." Some evidence is available that in the early part of the sixteenth century the bay may have been called "Bahia del Espiritu Santo," which means Bay of the Holy Spirit. In the latter part of that century, however, the French settlers used some form of the current name which they derived from the Mauvila Indians. Since the beginning of the eighteenth century all maps carried some form of the "Mobile Bay" name. A telephone survey conducted by the *Mobile Register* revealed some support for the name change, although it was not overwhelming. Nine-hundred and nine respondents registered support for changing the name to the "Bay of the Holy Spirit," whereas 772 registered opposition. In the process 18 callers suggested alternative names ranging from "Bay of Jimi Hendrix" to "Eastern Shore Cess Pool." Eventually the Alabama state names authority rejected the proposal as did the U.S. Board on Geographic Names. In doing so the Board pointed out how further investigation revealed that several communities around the bay did not favor the change, nor did Baldwin and Mobile Counties. All felt the name "Mobile Bay" to be not only unique, but well established.

Some recently named geographic features in the state of Utah include Thumb and Pinky Ridge. Since Finger Ridge, a physically similar feature, was already named, the proponent wished to continue the theme. Another proposal to name an unnamed sinkhole in Florida "Butters Lake" after the proponent's great-great grandfather was turned down because it did not satisfy all elements of the commemorative names policy. The name "Lake Oleo" was approved instead. That proposal was ostensibly made because Oleo Avenue runs along one side of the sinkhole.

Canada, too, experiences proposals to change familiar names of geographic features. Currently someone is attempting to gain support to recommend that Hudson Bay be renamed "Canada Sea." Some indigenous peoples have expressed opposition to the use of the word "squaw" in place names. The Canadian Permanent Committee on Geographical Names is dealing with this issue on a case-by-case basis.

Conclusion

Keeping track of the changes needed to update the world map, is not an easy task. It requires constant vigilance and demands awareness of conflicts among peoples and the resolutions to those conflicts as they occur. It calls for attention to new cooperative efforts among people and how those efforts might affect territorial divisions. It requires a willingness to search for the detailed information needed to update the maps that are to portray the new relationships. The reality behind many the changes is that some people's dreams have been realized, but not without exacting tolls in terms of human suffering and anguish, especially for those who were unable to hold on to their dreams in the struggle for territorial control.

Reference

Geography for Life: National Geography Standards 1994. Washington, D.C.: National Geographic Research and Exploration for the American Geographical Society, Association of American Geographers, National Council for Geographic Education, and the National Geographic Society.

Resource List

Access can be gained in the following ways through:

GOPHER: dosfan.lib.uic.edu

UNIVERSAL RESOURCE LOCATOR: gopher://dosfan.lib.uic.edu/

WORLD WIDE WEB: http://dosfan.lib.uic.edu/dosfan.html.

The Internet address is http://164.214.2.50/check_login.html.

A list of United Nations Publications can be obtained from the United Nations, Sales Section, New York, New York 10017.

Part IV: Educational Perspectives

CHAPTER 14.

THE DYNAMIC POLITICAL MAP: LEARNING ACTIVITIES

Alice T. M. Rechlin Perkins

Introduction: The dynamic political map is a manifestation of the conflict and cooperation among Earth's human population. The poem below provides not only a rhythmic account of some shifts of power on each of the continents plus Oceania, but also a powerful vehicle for further investigation. Analysis of the changing world map should lead to an understanding of the dynamics behind these changes.

Grade Level: Grades 9-12, college

Time Required: The time may vary from one class period to a semester project, depending upon how the teacher wishes to use the material.

National Geography Standards: Geography Standard 13, grades 9-12 and college (How the forces of cooperation and conflict among people influence the division and control of Earth's surface).

Skills: The learning activity requires students to apply the scientific method by asking geographic questions; acquiring, organizing and analyzing geographic information; and answering geographic questions.

Objectives: Students should acquire a detailed understanding of specific boundary and name changes that have occurred on the world political map, and should develop an appreciation of the powerful and dynamic effects that the forces of conflict and cooperation among peoples have upon the positioning of boundaries and the naming of places. They should be able to explain how the forces of conflict and cooperation lead to the allocation and reallocation of spatial control of portions of the Earth. Students should also develop a keener sense of the possible consequences of political disagreements and agreements, and should become more keenly aware of the human suffering and anguish that accompanies such changes.

Materials: World map with political boundaries and place names circa 1900, and contemporary world map with current political boundaries and place names; regional geography and history textbooks; access to current volumes of the *Statesman's Year-Book, World Almanac,* and *World Factbook*; access to *Border and Territorial Disputes* (Longman, 1992) and *Drawing the Line*, by Mark Monmonier (Henry Holt, 1995); access to an encyclopedia and other library or communication resources; the poem "As the World Turns it Chops Itself Up" (provided below).

As the World Turns it Chops Itself Up
by Alice Rechlin Perkins,
June 1996

O'er the vast expanse of Africa
 the map has been redrawn.
This century was indeed the one
 that gave it a new dawn.
So Cote d'Ivoire's not Ivory Coast
 and Burkina Faso's Volta's host
Namibia now its own does rule
 and also Walvis Bay so cool.

While to the south Morocco vies
    to cut it neighbor down to size.
French Africa, it did give sway
    to Chad and Niger on the way
Eritrea, a bud from its neighbor's hide
    leaves landlocked Ethiopia on the inside.
No longer can the Homelands taunt
    those who within them they did haunt.
And all the while gray elephants defy
    the lines that do us mystify.

Now Asia appears like another story,
    solid, unchanging in all its glory.
Look closer though and you'll see what
    lost territories that were ne'er forgot.
Before two thousand, like prodigal sons,
    Hong Kong and Macau will rejoin the Hans.
And while muscles may flex in the China seas
    to terrify the Taiwanese,
Countries vie for the Spratly's scant soil
    just to covet sea lanes and pools of oil.
Japan and Russia remain quite tense
    over the Kuril Islands that sit on the fence.
Indochina, you know, was once part of France.
    That's before the peoples took a tough stance.
Today they remain in three parts divided—
    Cambodia, Laos, and Vietnam united.
And the Union of Burma is now Myanmar
    wrought with problems galore that reach deep and far.
What, you may wonder, will come of East Timor.
    Will Indonesia ingest it forever more?
But the wall of great China, it doth still remain.
    A few things, you see, do stay the same.

Since the 1990s in the European realm
    new freedoms have been gained.
The Baltics, they began anew
    as did Moldova, Belarus, Ukraine.
Yet to the west the hope for union
    caused the Wall to tumble down,
And Germany, that once-torn land,
    regained its common ground.
But Czechoslovakia, like Humpty Dumpty,
    cracked and split in two.
While Yugoslavia to the south and east
    broke into five, that's true.
Today its parts are restless;
    old hatreds stir anew,
As Serbs and Croats do hunger
    for lands they might pursue.
And people died in Bosnia,

like pawns of kings and queens,
As leaders hold tenaciously
        to their territorial dreams.
Macedonia's name causes consternation;
        to Greece it amounts to expropriation.
As FYROM they would have it shown,
        since its acronym is little known.
Yet even with all this grist for schism,
        The European Union brings promise and vision.

Compare boundary lines in North America;
        they really seem quite stable.
But don't be fooled, there are some lines
        prove that to be a fable.
It's just that harsh negotiators
        have not gotten to their task
Of settling all the little claims
        that governments have asked.
Quebec's quest for independence
        causes a lot of agitation,
While Nunavut is waiting
        to complete its long gestation.
From Northwest Territories it will be born
        before the next millenium's dawn.
And in the U.S. citizens delight
        in naming places just for spite.
The names are colorful and fun
        They're pretty hard to be undone.
There's Bucksnort, Dumm Place, and Skunktown Plain,
        Hog Heaven, Do Stop, and Calamity Jane.
Names like Finger, Thumb, and Pinky Ridge
        match Rattlesnake, Accident, the Occoquan bridge.
And in Mexico just to the south
        huge Olmec heads do hide
Beneath the dust of later times
        when Spaniards turned the tide.
Well before the man, Columbus
        entered onto this world's scene
Thrived stone cities of the Inca
        with long highways in between.
They traversed the mighty Andes
        and swung down to the east
Connecting a vast empire
        of which they could well boast.
But Pizarro brought the people down
        and stole the gold for which they toiled.
And kings and queens and popes alike
        divided up the spoils.
Boundary lines were finally drafted;
        the continent sliced up into portions,
To lead the way for brand new states

from which intruders made their fortunes.
The British, Dutch, French, Portuguese
    arrived sometime thereafter
To stake out claims all on their own
    that would complicate things faster.
And so today we don't really know
    where Venezuela stops and starts,
And Suriname would have a chunk
    of Guyana's southern parts.
Some distance away, high in the hills,
    are Ecuador and Peru.
They've been at odds since viceroy times
    from whence their tensions grew.
Today they still get testy
    as old wounds begin to fester
From quarrels and disagreements
    that in vain they do sequester.
But all in all this abundant land
    gives the world astounding wealth
Its sky mountains yield us minerals
    and its lowland plants our health.

But that's not all, you might suspect.
    The Pacific is not placid yet.
While natives sailed the wide expanse
    and fire walkers warmed toes in dance
The Europeans came along
    with disease and weapons mighty strong.
They stole the lands, renamed them too,
    'til no one knew what belonged to who.
And Captain Cook sailed through the strait
    that bears his name to this very date.
Then against the currents to what became Botany Bay
    he found a land about which the king did say,
"We'll banish our prisoners down under the earth
    to fend for themselves for whatever it's worth."
But other Oceanic peoples, they fought back
    to gain the liberty that they lacked.
Today Samoa and Pitcairn Islands remain
    but others have no familiar name.
It's now Kirabati, not Gilbert and Ellice,
    since the people refused to render to Caesar.
Vanuatu replaced the New Hebrides
    to welcome freedom like an onshore breeze.

You know, it was only yesterday
    that trusted territories gave way.
And Palau with all its tiny lands
    became the world's newest sovereign sands.

Executing the Activity: Assign a different section of the poem that completes an idea to each student for independent investigation and explanation. See examples below.

Africa:
1. Identify a century of change by comparing a political map of Africa circa 1900 to a current political map.
2. Investigate the reasons for the name changes of Cote d'Ivoire and Volta.
3. What factors led to the separation of Eritrea from Ethiopia? How does this affect the economic geography of Ethiopia?
4. Investigate whether boundary changes over the last fifty years in the savanna regions of Africa may have altered the migrations and habitats of large game animals.

Asia
1. Investigate reasons behind tensions between China and Taiwan and the meaning behind the show of power by the People's Republic of China in the China Sea.
2. Identify countries that claim all or part of the Spratly Islands (central part of South China Sea, about 775 miles or 1247 kilometers northeast of Singapore) and describe the reasons for their claims.
3. Investigate tension between Russia and Japan over the Kuril Islands.
4. Examine the geopolitical history of Southeast Asia and explain the changing pattern of territorial control.

Europe
1. Compare a map of Europe in the 1980s to a current map. Identify the boundary changes that have occurred and identify those countries that have gained their independence since 1990.
2. Suggest reasons for the division of Czechoslovakia into the Czech Republic and Slovakia.
3. Examine the historical and cultural geography of the former Yugoslavia. How does knowledge of the cultural geography of the region lead to an understanding of the war in Bosnia and Herzegovina?

North America
1. Investigate the territorial changes and economic problems that might arise if Quebec were to secede from Canada.
2. What is the basis for the division of Canada's Northwest Territory and the creation of Nunavut?
3. Who were the Olmec? How are they related to the peoples of present-day Mexico?

South America
1. Map the extent of the Inca Empire, its major cities, and highways of communication.
2. Investigate boundary disputes between Guyana and Venezuela and between Guyana and Suriname. Were Guyana to lose both disputes, compare its territory as it would appear on the map with its territory today.
3. Trace the territorial dispute between Ecuador and Peru, and identify the reasons for it.

Australia and Oceania
1. Trace the migration patterns of the Polynesians, Micronesians, and Melanesians as they settled the islands of the Pacific Ocean.
2. Compare a political map of the Pacific from the first half of the twentieth century with a current map. Identify the name and sovereignty changes that took place.
3. Describe the processes leading to the recent independence of Palau.

Alternative Learning Opportunities

Place-name changes generally involve a good deal of debate. Yet there are methodical procedures and policies in place to recommend place-name changes for settlements and geographic features already named, or to recommend new names for unnamed features.

Option 1: Investigate the procedures and policies in place in your state for naming geographic features by contacting your State Names Authority.

Option 2: Investigate the procedures and policies that are in place at the federal level for naming geographic features by contacting the United States Board on Geographic Names, located within the United States Geological Survey.

Option 3: If there is a significant geographical feature that has no official name and that students wish to name, have the class follow the procedures and policies for naming it.

CHAPTER 15

EFFECTIVE WRITING ASSIGNMENTS IN TEACHING POLITICAL GEOGRAPHY

Arlene M. Shelley

Educators in geography and other disciplines have long recognized that writing assignments are effective means of promoting learning through active student participation. Writing assignments lead students through a self-directed discovery process. In undertaking writing assignments, students gather information, analyze material, and formulate responses to problems. Writing assignments present a unique opportunity for integrating and presenting knowledge and stimulating students' critical thinking.

The literature on higher education has suggested that many professors are reluctant to use writing assignments in their courses. Some professors believe that they do not have enough time or background to use writing assignments effectively, whereas others are doubtful that writing assignments contribute effectively to the learning process. Recent research has shown that these arguments do not apply to geography as a discipline. Relative to other academic disciplines, geography professors have embraced the use of writing assignments with enthusiasm.

A recent survey of geography professors across the United States indicated that nearly 80 percent of respondents assign writing to their undergraduate courses in geography (Shelley 1996). Statistical analysis revealed that the decision whether to assign writing was independent of the professor's age, tenure status, level of experience, and demographic characteristics. Rather, the only important factor predicting whether a given professor assigned writing was the nature of the course being taught.

Curricula in geography, as in other disciplines, can be divided between courses emphasizing low-level and high-level thinking. Low-level thinking emphasizes mastery of information and includes memorization of locations, dates, place names, and other facts. High-level thinking, by contrast, involves an active dialogue between the researcher and the subject matter under study. Students are expected to think critically and to organize, interpret, and analyze material, instead of relying on the memorization of factual information.

In the past, some geography educators have emphasized low-level thinking in their teaching. More recently, many geography educators have begun to call attention to the distinction between low-level and high-level thinking. Porter (1989: 52) has argued that teachers of geography should develop assignments that encourage understanding of the "complex relationships that animate modern geographical inquiry." Other writers on geographic education have also supported this emphasis on critical thinking (Sublett 1991; Rugg 1991; Winchell and Elder 1992).

The survey determined that virtually all of the geography professors who taught courses emphasizing high-level thinking assigned writing, whereas only half of those teaching courses emphasizing low-level thinking did so. For this reason, most professors teaching courses in human geography, environmental geography, and the geography of particular regions required writing of their students whereas many professors teaching world geography, physical geography, and techniques regarded their mission as emphasizing mastery rather than interpretation and chose not to assign writing.

How does political geography fit within this framework? Relative to other sub-fields within geography, teaching political geography emphasizes high-level thinking. Political geography students cannot learn the material by relying on memorization. Rather, they must learn to interpret current events, relate them to their life experiences, and be able to articulate and defend their opinions concerning possible policy options. These considerations illustrate that the design of effective writing assignments is of great importance to teaching political geography successfully.

What types of writing assignments are especially effective in courses dealing with aspects of political geography at the college and pre-college levels? Why are these assignments valuable? This chapter will address these questions. First, it presents a conceptual model of appropriate writing in geography as a discipline. This conceptual framework is then applied to the sub-discipline of political geography. Finally, it presents and discusses examples of successful writing assignments used in contemporary political geography classes.

A Conceptual Framework for Effective Writing Assignments

Shelley (1996) has developed a conceptual framework for use by teachers to promote and encourage the use of effective writing assignments. The conceptual framework identifies three stages to the writing process. First, how does the student obtain the information needed to complete the assignment? Second, how does the student process this information? Finally, how is the final product prepared and presented? The choice among alternative approaches to each of these questions can and should be linked to course objectives.

A variety of sources are available to students completing writing assignments. Some professors rely on the personal life experiences of students, whereas others require the collection of facts or other information from primary or secondary sources. Students can obtain information through fieldwork, interviews, and from published sources including newspapers, magazines, and books.

Today, the Internet has become an increasingly valuable source of information for students obtaining information for writing assignments. Newspapers, television and radio stations, and even individual countries retain and update sites on the World Wide Web. These enable students to obtain information about many current events of interest to teachers and students of political geography. For example, major newspapers throughout the United States maintain websites that allow access to state- and county-level electoral data. Relevant information about boundary disputes, environmental problems, and ethnic conflicts in trouble spots throughout the world can also be accessed through the Internet and World Wide Web.

What does a student do with this information? As Shelley's (1996) conceptual framework has indicated, teachers can differentiate writing assignments on the basis of how the student processes the information once obtained. Some assignments require students to use information to solve problems. Other assignments expect them to describe or explain processes and procedures. Other analyses involve comparison and contrast. A fourth category includes writing assignments that require students to define and advocate a position on an important or controversial subject.

Teachers have used effectively all of these various types of writing assignments in political geography. Problem-solving assignments might include interpretations of election outcomes, suggested methods for the delineation of electoral districts, or proposals to resolve boundary disputes between countries. The second category might include assignments requiring a student to describe the activities of a United Nations agency or the development of a particular foreign or military policy.

The latter two categories are used even more frequently in political geography teaching than in other subjects. Teachers have often assigned comparison and contrast papers to political geography students in response to interesting and controversial questions. For example, why has the breakup of Yugoslavia been associated with so much bloodshed whereas the Soviet Union and Czechoslovakia broke up relatively peacefully? How do the environmental policies of different countries compare and why? Assigning students, individually or in groups, to obtain information about important crisis points in the contemporary world and use this information to compare and contrast places or events often provides a useful starting point for effective writing assignments.

In other cases, assigning students to identify and defend positions on controversial issues is an effective means of promoting synthesis of course material. For example, teachers can ask their students to defend their positions on controversial issues such as rainforest depletion, immigration, or international trade. An effective means of doing this is to ask students to articulate and defend a proposed policy, perhaps by playing the role of an advisor to the government of the United States or another country.

A most effective assignment obtained in the survey was developed for a course on the geography of non-Western cultures. As discussed in more detail below, this assignment may be equally relevant to political geography. Each student in the class was assigned a non-Western, less developed country and then asked to assume the role of a development officer who is responsible for planning future economic development for the assigned country. Students then use various resources to obtain information about the country and then complete papers in which they articulate an appropriate economic development strategy for the country.

Assignments requiring advocacy can also be linked with prediction. For example, teachers can assign students to predict the outcomes of current events such as elections, legal controversies, or international disputes and use appropriate factual material to defend and justify their predictions. Teachers can also follow such assignments with a later assignment in which students evaluate the success or failure of their predictions in retrospect. For example, students can be asked to predict the outcome of a Presidential election on a local, state, or regional basis before Election Day. Based on information obtained from newspapers, magazines, the Internet, and other sources, which candidate is likely to carry each state and why? After the election, a second assignment asks the students to evaluate the accuracy of their predictions.

The third element of the conceptual framework involves the nature of the final product. Shelley's survey indicated that the most common type of writing assignment geography professors used was the term paper. Some professors assigned alternatives such as short reaction papers, journals or logbooks, creative writing assignments, and photographic essays. Regardless of the specific form of the final product, however, it is important to distinguish between what Winchell and Elder (1992) have termed Type A and Type B writing. Type A writing is explanatory writing, or writing that "transmits existing information and ideas" (Winchell and Elder 1992: 273-274). Type B writing, in contrast, is exploratory and emphasizes creativity and synthesis rather than the structured presentation of information.

In political geography, effective writing assignments are likely to combine both types of writing. For example, a paper describing a particular international conflict situation such as that of the former Zaire or Bosnia would be Type A writing. On the other hand, an essay that predicts the effects of diplomatic solutions to such conflicts would be Type B writing. Although Winchell and Elder argue that the effective integration of writing-to-learn methods into geography curricula requires that students be challenged to reach beyond Type A writing into Type B writing, students must first use Type A writing to present the facts underlying the positions that they advocate.

Applying the Conceptual Framework to Political Geography

How can we apply the conceptual framework to teaching political geography? In this section, we address this question by presenting a few examples of successful writing assignments used in contemporary political geography classes and linking them to the conceptual framework.

Teachers can easily and effectively adapt the development-officer assignment described briefly earlier in this chapter can be adapted to political geography courses. Political geography textbooks have paid increasing attention to world-systems theory and related approaches to international economic development as organizing principles (i.e., Demko and Wood 1994, Taylor 1993). The world-systems perspective emphasizes uneven development, implying that exchange between different areas often has the effect of benefiting more developed areas at the expense of less developed ones. Through colonialism, the world economy diffused from its European origins to other parts of the world. Differences in levels of development remained significant even after former European colonies in Asia, Africa, and elsewhere achieved political independence in the years after World War II.

In recent years, increased attention has been paid to how international trade and the activities of Western-based transnational corporations affect the economies of less developed countries. Proponents of the interests of the less developed countries generated the concept of the New International Economic Order. This concept suggests that the international community has a moral obligation to intervene in order to improve conditions in less developed countries. Advocates of the New International Economic Order have tried, with varying degrees of success, to reorient global politics from the East-West perspective associated with the Cold War to a North-South perspective emphasizing differences between the developed and the less developed countries.

To the extent that the economic processes associated with the world economy continue to benefit the North at the expense of the South, leaders of less developed countries face difficult choices. Given the dominance of international trade by developed countries, and given the increasingly important role of transnational corporations in the global economy, how can less developed countries develop without falling farther and farther behind the developed countries? Playing the role of a development officer gives the political geography student an opportunity to address these questions while learning about particular countries in greater detail.

To complete this assignment successfully, a student (or group of students) must rely heavily on obtaining useful, accurate information. Two types of information are needed: information about the country itself, and information about the relationships between the country and the changing global economy. This information must then be linked to knowledge about the development process itself.

Students can obtain the information needed to complete this assignment from several different sources. They can obtain basic knowledge about the country and its economy, resources. and physical geography from encyclopedias and other standard reference works, yet we should warn students not to rely solely on such compendia. Instead, we should encourage them to use original source material. Articles in newspapers, periodicals, and the Internet are prime source material for the relevant information. Effective information processing is essential to the successful completion of this assignment. The student must also link information about the country's resources, economic conditions, and other characteristics to knowledge of the world economy and development theory to describe and advocate a proposed development policy effectively

Within the conceptual framework described above, completing the development officer assignment requires an advocacy style of writing. Advocacy is difficult for some high school and college students, for two reasons. Many students are reluctant to voice opinions, particularly when fearful that their opinions may differ from those of the instructor. Students sometimes express concern that they will receive lower grades if they advocate a distinctive or unusual position. In such cases, teachers should remind students that their grade will be determined by the quality with which they defend their opinions and not solely by the content of the opinions.

Not only are students sometimes reluctant to express their opinions but some have difficulty with the idea that advocacy does not lead to an unequivocally correct answer. Students unfamiliar with geography and other social sciences sometimes fail to grasp the fact that no one opinion, as long as it is reasonably presented and defended, is inherently better than another. Students majoring in business, sciences, or engineering are especially likely to express this concern, because conceptual thinking and associated writing tasks in these disciplines emphasize the search for a single correct or best answer to the exclusion of others. Teachers should caution students completing this or other advocacy-oriented assignments that advocating a particular position is an intellectual effort distinct from the search for a correct solution to a problem.

Completing the assignment involves a combination of Type A and Type B writing. The student must use Type A writing in describing the country and its resources and development prospects, but students can use Type B writing in describing and justifying the proposed development policies.

Using Writing Assignments to Follow Elections

A second approach to writing is to develop a sequence of writing assignments over the course of a semester. An example of this concept involves asking students to follow, describe, and evaluate an election campaign or other significant political issue as it unfolds over time. Here, we illustrate this idea with reference to a proposed sequence of assignments in which students describe American Presidential elections. This proposed sequence is appropriate for political geography courses held in the fall semester (or fall quarter) of a traditional academic calendar. The sequence may also be relevant to local and state elections or other sequential current events.

The proposed assignment sequence includes completing three papers. In the first paper, completed during the campaign, students describe and interpret campaign strategies of one or more parties or candidates. For example, students may be asked to map and interpret the locational decisions made by presidential candidates during specified campaign periods. Where did the candidates appear? What subjects were emphasized in their speeches?

In the second paper, students predict the outcome of elections on a state-by-state basis. Because of the structure of the Electoral College, American presidential elections can be conceptualized as a combination of 51 separate state elections (Shelley *et al.* 1996). Students are assigned to predict the outcome of the election in each state or region and justify their predictions on the basis of the interface between local and national considerations. Students should complete and hand in this assignment shortly before Election Day.

After the election is over and the ballots are counted, students are given the final assignment in the sequence. In this final essay, students are assigned to discuss the election outcomes. In doing so, they compare their predictions with the results and evaluate the accuracy of their predictions. In light of the events, the students might also be assigned to hazard predictions about future events.

Students can use many sources of information to complete this assignment. Local and national news media are important sources of information. The national newspaper *USA Today* prints information about the whereabouts of each major-party presidential and vice-presidential candidate each day during the campaign. National newspapers such as *USA Today*, the *New York Times*, and the *Washington Post*, daily local newspapers, and news magazines such as *Newsweek, Time*, and *U.S. News* and *World Report* publish state-by-state predictions concerning election outcomes. All of these sources provide extensive post-election coverage, which often emphasizes interpretation of the outcome on a regional basis. The Internet is an increasingly valuable source of information as well. Major political parties and candidates create websites, and newspaper articles and other analyses from around the country are also available.

The information processing and writing skills associated with completing this assignment vary across the sequence. To complete the first paper, students must obtain, map, and interpret the movements and campaign strategies of the political parties. The second and third papers require more complex information processing skills. Students must not only present information obtained from original sources such as those described above but they must also use this information to make their own predictions. As in the case of the development officer assignment, teachers must caution students that their predictions need not be identical, but they must justified on the basis of reasonable arguments.

The three papers form an effective sequence between Type A and Type B writing. The first paper, in which the student describes the movements and campaign strategies of presidential candidates, emphasizes Type A writing. The second and third papers combine Type A writing with Type B writing. An additional advantage of this sequence of papers is that it helps generate student interest in elections and other current events. Students often pride themselves on the accuracy of their predictions and keep their prediction maps handy while watching returns on election night.

A third writing assignment used effectively in political geography classes involves the ranking of countries based on geopolitical importance. Archer *et al.* (1997) provide details of this assignment in a recent paper and point out that contemporary geopolitical transition may have profound effects on teaching political geography. The Cold War, which dominated global geopolitics for nearly half a century following World War II, shaped the geopolitical worldviews of most teachers. For students who were still children when the Berlin Wall was torn down, the Cold War is a period of time studied in history class rather than a major influence on their lives and modes of thinking.

Recognizing the differing effects of the Cold War on the thinking of students and teachers, Archer *et al.* (1997) administered surveys to political geography classes in Nebraska, Texas, and Florida. In the survey, they asked students to rank the 55 countries of the world whose populations exceed 15 million in order of "geopolitical importance." The original article by Archer *et al.* (1997) includes details of the survey results and their implications for teaching geopolitics. Here, we focus on the writing assignment associated with the survey.

The three professors who administered the questionnaire assigned the students to write essays justifying their rankings. The assignment encouraged students to consider what characteristics were associated with ranking some countries as more important than others. This task required students to obtain information about the countries under consideration and link this information to knowledge of geopolitics, which the students had obtained in lectures, readings, and other classroom activities.

How does this assignment fit within our conceptual framework? As in the other assignments, information about the places to be ranked is critical to its successful completion. After considering criteria such as location, population, level of economic development, economic bases, and natural resources, students must then determine how the countries compare with one another on relevant criteria. This task requires students to consult standard reference sources, journalistic accounts, and published and on-line information sources such as those described above.

Information processing involves linking the information about the countries to the criteria. This can be done quantitatively, for example, by computing an index of importance based on real data about important criteria. Some students prefer a more qualitative approach to ranking the countries. Having obtained the information, the student must then write about how he or she selected and applied his or her criteria, and how they ranked the countries according to the criteria. As in the other two assignments, the successful completion of this exercise requires an effective combination of Type A and Type B writing. Type A writing is used in identifying the criteria and describing the characteristics of individual countries relative to these criteria, whereas Type B writing is needed for the student to link the criteria and the predictions.

Conclusion

Effective writing assignments are critical to teaching political geography. A survey of geography professors in the United States revealed that nearly all of those who teach courses involving some form of higher-order thinking, including political geography courses, use writing assignments in their courses.

In this paper, a conceptual framework based on Shelley's (1996) analysis of writing assignments in geography courses was developed and applied to political geography. The analysis suggests that effective writing assignments are those that encourage students to obtain information from original sources, process this information to advocate positions, or make predictions, and combine Type A and Type B writing techniques to present the results of their analyses effectively. Such an approach to writing will allow teachers of political geography to integrate knowledge of this important subject with the development of essential skills in written communication.

References

Archer, J. C., F. M. Shelley, and J. I. Leib 1997. "The Perceived Geopolitical Importance of the Countries of the World," *Journal of Geography (96): 76-83.*

Demko, G. J. and W. B. Wood 1994. *Reordering the World: Geopolitical Perspectives on the Twenty-first Century.* Boulder, Colo.: Westview.

Porter, P. 1989. "In Dunkelsten, Africa: Africa in the Student Mind," *Journal of Geography,* (88): 51-58.

Rugg, D. 1991. "Making Introductory Cultural Geography More Relevant," *Journal of Geography* (90): 219-221.

Shelley, A. M. 1996. *The Use of Writing in Contemporary Geography Courses in the United States,* unpublished Ph.D. dissertation, Department of Geography, University of Oklahoma, Norman.

Shelley, F. M., J. C. Archer, F. M. Davidson, and S. D. Brunn 1996. *The Political Geography of the United States.* New York: Guilford.

Sublett, M. D. 1991. "Incorporating Student Logbooks into Geography Classes," *Journal of Geography* (90): 50-54.

Winchell, D., and D. Elder 1992. "Writing in the Geography Curriculum," *Journal of Geography* (91): 273-276

CHAPTER 16
REDISTRICTING ELECTORAL SPACE: A CASE STUDY OF U.S. CONGRESSIONAL DISTRICTS IN GEORGIA
Scott R. Myers

The United States Constitution requires that a national population census be taken every ten years to determine how many seats to which each state is entitled in the U.S. House of Representatives. Population shifts among states result in redistricting and reapportionment of the electoral districts inside many of our states after each census. The state legislatures or on special occasions the courts draw congressional district boundary lines within states to determine the scope and the shape of each congressional district. This set of activities should help students develop an understanding of the wide range of phenomena that influence the geography of congressional redistricting. The state of Georgia provides an excellent case study of redistricting. After the 1990 census the U.S. Supreme Court declared its new 11th district unconstitutional requiring Georgia to redraw its congressional districts a second time. This lesson focuses on the array of political, social, economic, and spatial factors that influence the complex decision-making process when states redraw political district boundaries to comply with the guidelines of the high court.

Grade Level: Grades 9-12

Time required: 2 to 4 class periods.

National Geography Standards*: (appropriate pages cited from the standards, grades 9- 12)
1. How to use maps and other geographic representations, tools, and technologies to acquire, process, and report information from a spatial perspective. 184-185
3. How to analyze the spatial organization of people, places, and the environments on Earth's surface. 188-189
4. The physical and human characteristics of places. 190-191
5. That people create regions to interpret Earth's complexity. 192-194
9. The characteristics, distribution, and migration of human populations on Earth's surface. 201-202
11. The patterns and networks of economic interdependence on Earth's surface. 206-207
13. How the forces of cooperation and conflict among people influence the division and control of earth's surface. 210-211
18. How to apply geography to interpret the present and plan for the future. 221-222

---

* *Geography for Life: National Geography Standards 1994.* Washington, D.C.: National Geographic Research and Exploration for the American Geographical Society, Association of American Geographers, National Council for Geographic Education, and the National Geographic Society. (Available from the National Council for Geographic Education, 16A Leonard Hall, Indiana University of Pennsylvania, Indiana, PA 15705, $7.00 plus postage and handling.)

Vocabulary: census, choropleth map, gerrymander, Miller v. Johnson 1995, redistricting, Reynolds v. Sims 1964, Voting Rights Act of 1965

Objectives:
· Students will compare past and present congressional district maps of Georgia to analyze the historic patterns of spatial organization.
· Students will design a population choropleth map with five classes.
· Students will design a racial majority-minority choropleth map.
· Students will take into consideration political, economic, and cultural factors in making geo-

graphic decisions.
· Students will design congressional district maps using political, economic, cultural, and spatial criteria.
· Students will compare and contrast their congressional district map with the one drawn by the district court in 1995.

Materials:
· Outline Map of Georgia (Handout 1)
· Maps of Congressional Districts in Georgia for 1995, 1992-1995, 1950, 1970, and 1980 (Handouts 2, 3, 4, 5, 6)
· Map of Counties in Georgia (Handout 7)
· Index to Counties in Georgia (Handout 8)
· Political Map of Georgia with Interstate Highways (Handout 9)
· Political, Economic, Cultural, and Spatial Background sheet (Handout 10)
· Political, Economic, Cultural, and Spatial Background response sheet (Handout 11)
· Congressional Maps through Time response sheet (Handout 12)
· U.S. Census Population Figures for Georgia Counties. Suggested Sources include Almanacs, U.S. Census Materials, or U.S. Atlas Software.
· Box of colored pencils

The Learning Activity:
Background
The House of Representatives in the United States Congress is an example of an elected legislature. Legislative representation is usually based on territorial groupings of the general population. The members of the House of Representatives are elected from 435 single-member districts that represent the total population in all fifty states. Each state gets one House member regardless of its population. Beyond that, the states are given representation on the basis of their specific population. The U.S. Constitution requires that a census be taken every ten years to determine how many seats to which each state is entitled in the House of Representatives. Within states, state legislatures draw congressional district boundary lines or in special occasions district courts will do so. Reapportionment and redistricting occurs, where necessary, after each decennial census. As a result of shifting populations, some states gain seats whereas other states lose seats in these reapportionments.

In 1789, the first House of Representatives had 59 members that represented 59 single-member districts in the thirteen original states. As new states entered the Union and the population of the U.S. increased, the size of the House grew through the years. In 1912, by act of Congress, membership was stabilized at the current figure of 435. At the present time, as a result of the 1990 census, a House member in each of the 435 single member districts, has an average of 572,000 constituents.

In Georgia, after the 1990 census, the state's representation increased from ten congressional seats to eleven congressional seats. Georgia gained one congressional seat because of population growth attributed to population shifts in the Sunbelt during the 1980s. As a result, the Georgia state legislature had to redraw its congressional districts.

The new congressional map was in accordance U.S. Department of Justice guidelines, which had the obligation of enforcing Voting Rights Act (VRA) of 1965. The new congressional map created three African-American majority districts. One of three districts was the strangely shaped 11th district, which included the state's rural African-American population majority core area in Middle Georgia with African-American populations in Augusta, Savannah, and suburban Atlanta. The United States Supreme Court ruled in (*Miller v. Johnson* 1995), that the 11th district was unconstitutional because race was the predominant force in determining the congressional district over all other political, economic, and spatial factors.

Introducing the Activity

The students will participate in a simulation as a group of geographers who are serving as consultants for the District Court's special panel to redraw the state of Georgia's congressional districts. Prior to the panel's meeting, the courts have declared Georgia's 11th congressional unconstitutional because of racial gerrymandering. The Georgia state legislature met in a special session to redraw congressional districts but the result was a political stalemate. The District Court was left with the task of redrawing congressional districts using political, economic, cultural, and spatial guidelines handed down by the Supreme Court in (*Miller v. Johnson* 1995). The geographers will incorporate the Supreme Court's guidelines and redraw the congressional districts in Georgia for the District Court to implement.

Provide an overview of the Learning Activity using the background information provided. First, outline the geography of The House of Representatives in the United States Congress; second, present the nature of the problem with the congressional districts in Georgia; third, introduce the simulation.

Executing the Activity

Divide the class into groups of three to five students, each group will simulate a team of geographers who are serving as consultants for the District Court's special panel to redraw the state of Georgia's congressional districts. Each team will complete a sequence of activities using geographic techniques to develop an understanding of the political, economic, cultural, and spatial guidelines handed down by the Supreme Court in (Miller v. Johnson 1995). Then each team will redraw the congressional districts in Georgia for the District Court to implement.

Activity One: Place Location in Georgia

Distribute Handout 1 and the colored pencils. Have each group: circle the city of Atlanta in blue, circle the cities of Albany, Athens, Augusta, Columbus, Macon, and Savannah in green, and trace interstate highways in red.

This map will provide a tool in the analysis in Activity Two.

Activity Two: Congressional Maps through Time in Georgia

Distribute the maps of Congressional Districts in Georgia for 1950, 1970, 1980, and 1990 (Handouts 3-6). Explain that these maps display the congressional districts that were a result of the decennial census for each year. Ask the students to analyze the four congressional maps with the place-location map and complete the questions on the Congressional Maps through Time response sheet (Handout 12).

Review the information from the Congressional Maps Through Time response sheet. Solicit responses from each group and combine the data of each group. Emphasize the spatial patterns of congressional district boundaries based on tradition.

Activity Three: Constructing Choropleth Maps

Distribute two copies of Counties in Georgia map (Handout 7). Explain the concept of a choropleth map.[1] Emphasize how geographers apply a spatial perspective to display differences in quantities.

Choropleth map #1 will focus on population density in Georgia. Using the county census data, divide the range of counties' population density into five to eight categories. Each category is then assigned a color or shading pattern, and each area on the map is colored based on its category of population density. This map will help with the grouping of counties into the eleven congression-

---

[1] A choropleth map results from coloring or shading ranges of quantities, e.g., population, population density [50-100 people per square mile or square kilometer, population range [50,000-100,000], or classes of percentages [50-60 percent], *within an existing political or human-made boundary* such as a country, state, county, or other minor civil division such as a congressional district.

al districts that should be uniform in population.

Choropleth map #2 will focus on African-American population density in Georgia. Using the county census data, divide the counties' population into two categories, counties with an African-American majority in population and counties with an African-American minority in population. Each category is then assigned a color or shading pattern, and each area on the map is colored based on its classification of African-American population density. This map will help with identifying counties to create majority African-American congressional districts that incorporate the Justice Department's guidelines under the Voting Rights Act.

Activity Four: Political, Economic, Cultural, and Spatial Background

Distribute Political, Economic, Cultural, and Spatial Background Sheet (Handout 10) and the corresponding response sheet (Handout 11). Ask the students to analyze the four summaries and complete the questions on the Political, Economic, Cultural and Spatial Background response sheet.

Review the information from the Background Response Sheet. Solicit responses from each group and combine the data of each group. Emphasize the guidelines for redrawing congressional; districts in Georgia.

Activity Five: Redrawing the Congressional Districts in Georgia

Taking into consideration the following Supreme Court guidelines in (Miller v. Johnson 1995), the students will draw the new congressional map for the state of Georgia based on the following political, economic, cultural and spatial criteria.

Supreme Court's Criteria:
1. Create eleven congressional districts in the state of Georgia.
2. Each congressional district needs to be approximately uniform in population with a range of 575,000 to 600,000 people per district.
3. Political gerrymandering is prohibited.
4. Create a majority-African-American congressional district to comply with VRA without racial gerrymandering.
5. Based on the concept "communities of interest," keep Georgia's four traditional economic *corner* districts intact and comply to the basic pattern observed from the maps of Congressional Districts in Georgia for 1950, 1970, 1980, and 1990.
6. Create a new congressional district based on the emergence of a new "community of interest" as a product of urban growth pushing from the metropolitan Atlanta region toward the northeast along the Interstate 85 corridor.
7. Preserve whole counties within the districts. You can make an exception in one of metropolitan Atlanta districts because of the difficulty of creating uniform population divisions.

Evaluation

After each team completes its congressional map, evaluate it with a checklist derived from activities 1-4, checking each team's place-location map, choropleth maps, and response sheets. Activities 1-4 can be worth 50 points.

Evaluate the Congressional map with a checklist based on the compliance of Supreme Court's Criteria. The synthesis map can be worth 40 points

Distribute the Congressional Map for Georgia drawn by the U.S. District Court in December of 1995. Have each team prepare either an oral or written summary that compares and contrasts their map with the one drawn by the U.S. District Court.

Reference

Leib, Jonathan I. 1998. "Political Geography and Voting Rights in the United States." Chapter 8 in F. M. Davidson, J. I. Leib, F. M. Shelley, G. R. Webster, eds., *Teaching Political Geography*. Indiana, Pa.: National Council for Geographic Education.

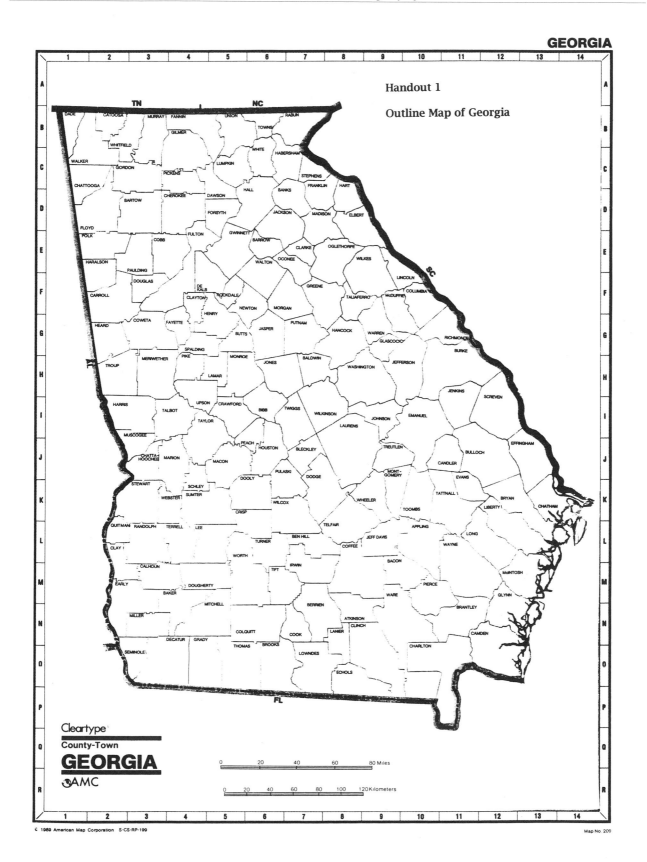

GEORGIA

Handout 1

Outline Map of Georgia

Cleartype

County-Town

GEORGIA

AMC

Map No. 209

Handout 2

Georgia Congressional Districts as Drawn by the U.S. District Court

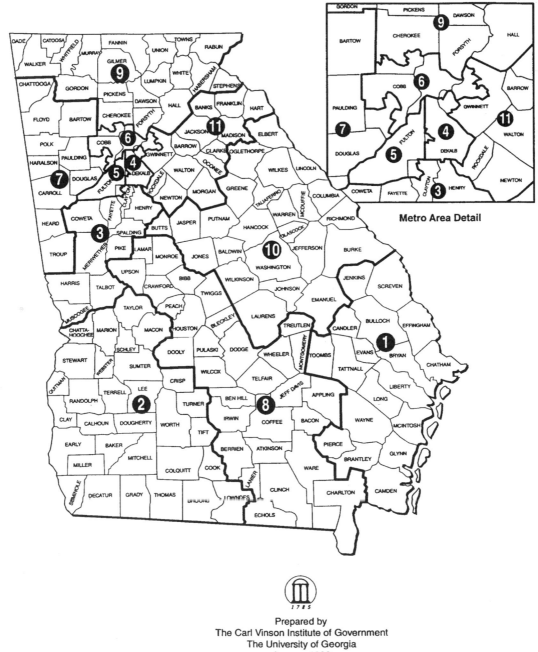

Metro Area Detail

Prepared by
The Carl Vinson Institute of Government
The University of Georgia
January 1996

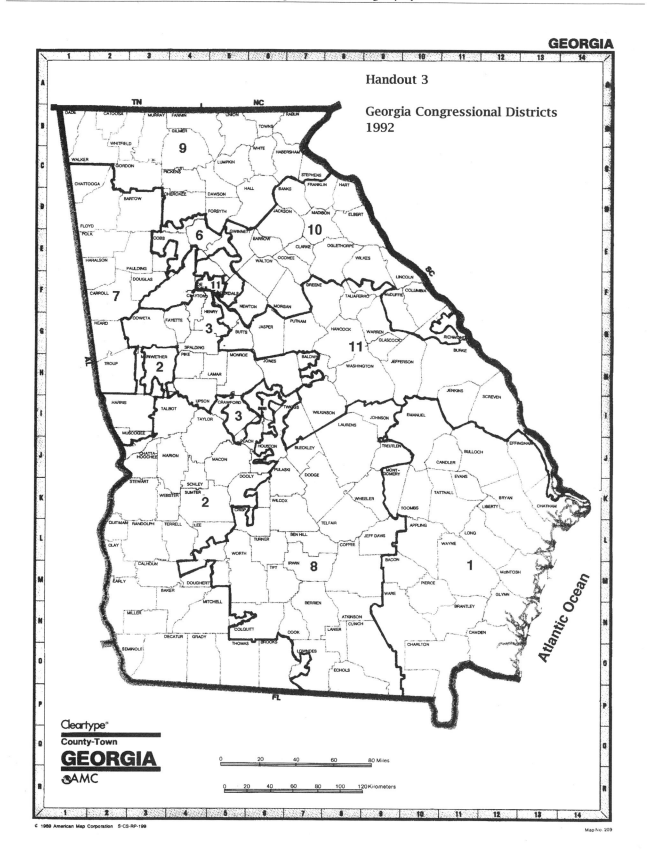

Handout 3

Georgia Congressional Districts
1992

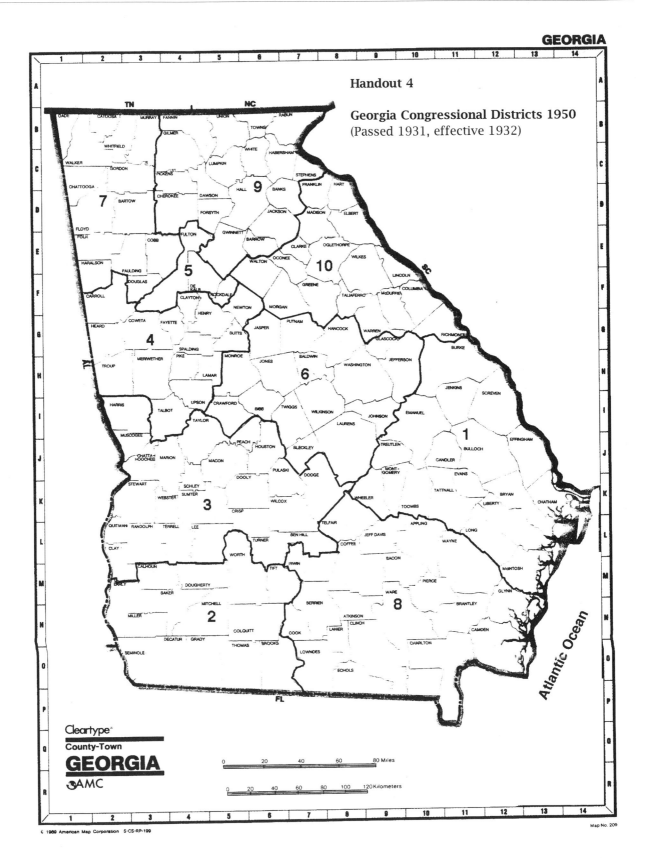

Handout 4

Georgia Congressional Districts 1950
(Passed 1931, effective 1932)

Cleartype
County-Town
GEORGIA
AMC

0   20   40   60   80 Miles

0   20   40   60   80   100   120 Kilometers

© 1989 American Map Corporation S-CS-RP-199

Map No. 209

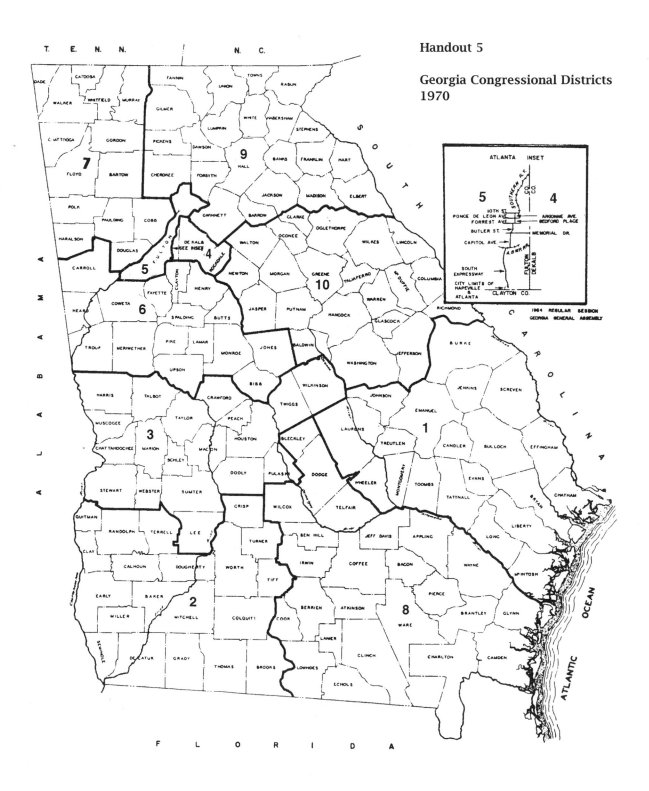

Handout 5

Georgia Congressional Districts
1970

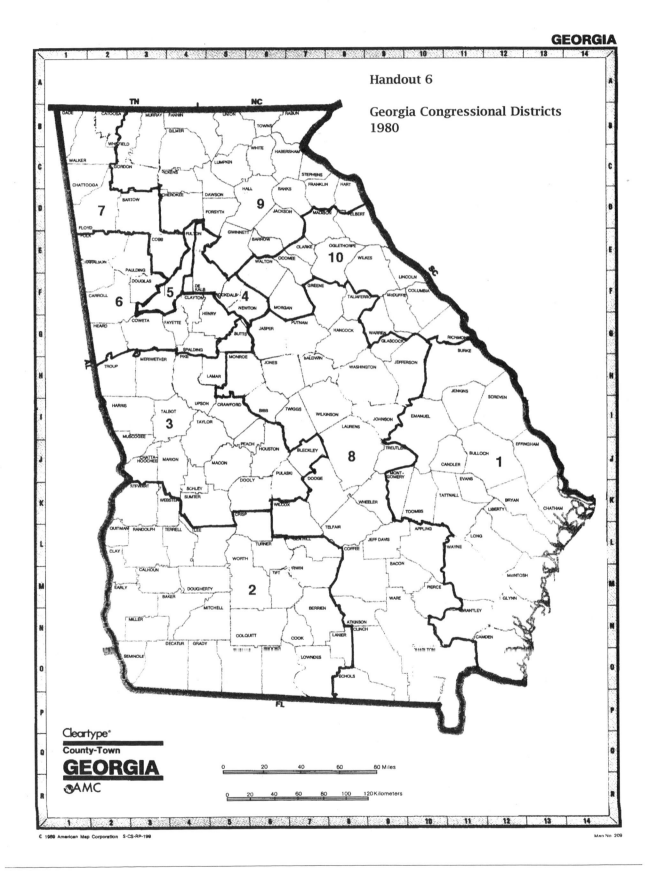

Handout 6

Georgia Congressional Districts
1980

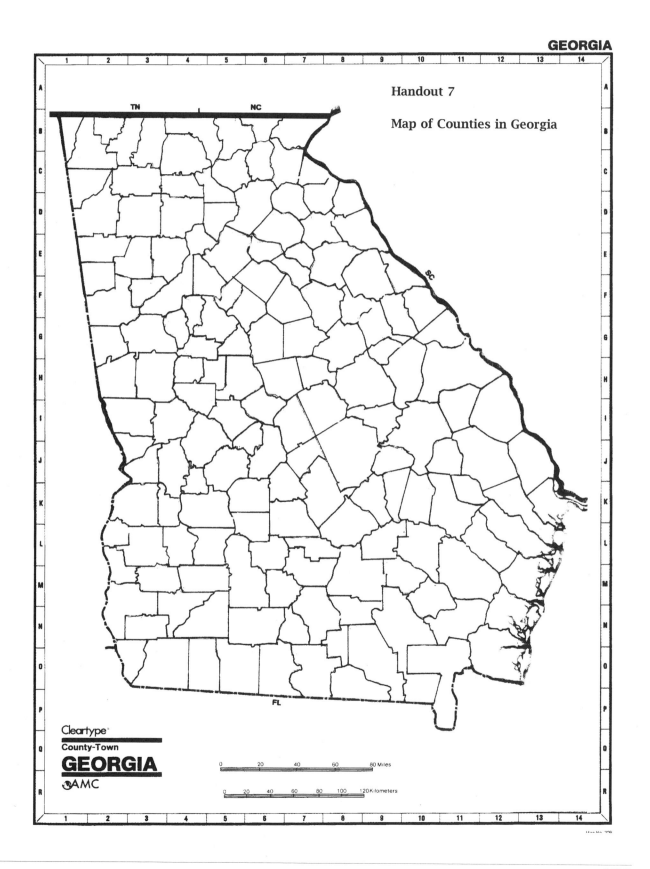

GEORGIA

Handout 7

Map of Counties in Georgia

Cleartype
County-Town
GEORGIA
AMC

Handout 8
Index to Counties in Georgia

APPLING	L-10	EVANS	J-11	NEWTON	F-5		
ATKINSON	N-8	FANNIN	B-4	OCONEE	E-6		
BACON	L-9	FAYETTE	F-4	OGELTHORPE	E-8		
BAKER	M-3	FLOYD	D-1	PAULDING	E-3		
BALDWIN	H-7	FORSYTH	D-5	PEACH	J-5		
BANKS	D-6	FRANKLIN	C-7	PICKENS	C-3		
BARROW	E-6	FULTON	E-4	PIERCE	M-10		
BARTOW	D-2	GILMER	B-4	PIKE	H-4		
BEN HILL	L-7	GLASCOCK	G-9	POLK	E-1		
BERRIEN	N-7	GLYNN	M-12	PULASKI	K-6		
BIBB	I-6	GORDON	C-2	PUTNAM	G-7		
BLECKLEY	J-7	GRADY	N-4	QUITMAN	L-2		
BRANTLEY	N-11	GREENE	F-7	RABUN	B-7		
BROOKS	N-6	GWINNETT	E-5	RANDOLPH	L-3		
BRYAN	K-12	HABERSHAM	C-6	RICHMOND	G-11		
BULLOCH	J-11	HALL	D-5	ROCKDALE	F-5		
BURKE	G-11	HANCOCK	G-8	SCHLEY	K-4		
BUTTS	G-5	HARALSON	E-1	SCREVEN	I-12		
CALHOUN	M-3	HARRIS	I-2	SEMINOLE	O-2		
CAMDEN	N-11	HART	C-8	SPALDING	G-4		
CANDLER	J-10	HEARD	G-2	STEPHENS	C-7		
CARROLL	F-2	HENRY	F-4	STEWART	K-3		
CATOOSA	B-2	HOUSTON	J-6	SUMTER	K-4		
CHARLTON	O-10	IRWIN	M-7	TALBOT	I-3		
CHATHAM	K-13	JACKSON	D-6	TALIAFERRO	F-6		
CHATTAHOOCHEE	J-3	JASPER	G-6	TATNALL	K-10		
CHATTOOGA	C-1	JEFF DAVIS	L-9	TAYLOR	I-4		
CHEROKEE	D-3	JEFFERSON	H-9	TELFAIR	L-8		
CLARKE	E-7	JENKINS	H-11	TERRELL	L-3		
CLAY	L-2	JOHNSON	I-9	THOMAS	O-5		
CLAYTON	F-4	JONES	H-6	TIFT	M-6		
CLINCH	N-6	LAMAR	H-5	TOOMBS	K-10		
COBB	E-4	LANIER	N-8	TOWNS	B-6		
COFFEE	L-8	LAURENS	I-8	TREUTLEN	J-9		
COLQUITT	N-5	LEE	L-4	TROUP	H-2		
COLUMBIA	F-10	LIBERTY	K-12	TURNER	L-6		
COOK	N-7	LINCOLN	F-9	TWIGGS	I-7		
COWETA	G-3	LONG	L-11	UNION	B-5		
CRAWFORD	I-5	LOWNDES	O-7	UPSON	I-4		
CRISP	K-5	LUMPKIN	C-5	WALKER	C-1		
DADE	B-1	MACON	J-8	WALTON	E-6		
DAWSON	D-5	MADISON	D-7	WARE	M-9		
DEKALB	E-4	MARION	J-3	WARREN	G-9		
DECATUR	N-4	MCDUFFIE	D-7	WASHINGTON	H-8		
DODGE	J-7	MCINTOSH	J-3	WAYNE	L-11		
DOOLY	J-5	MERIWETHER	F-6	WEBSTER	K-3		
DOUGHERTY	M-4	MILLER	N-3	WHEELER	K-6		
DOUGLAS	F-3	MITCHELL	N-4	WHITE	C-6		
EARLY	M-2	MONROE	H-5	WHITFIELD	D-2		
ECHOLS	O-8	MONTGOMERY	J-9	WILCOX	L-7		
EFFINGHAM	J-12	MORGAN	F-6	WILKES	E-6		
ELBERT	D-8	MURRAY	B-3	WILKINSON	I-7		
EMANUEL	I-10	MUSCOGEE	I-2	WORTH	L-5		

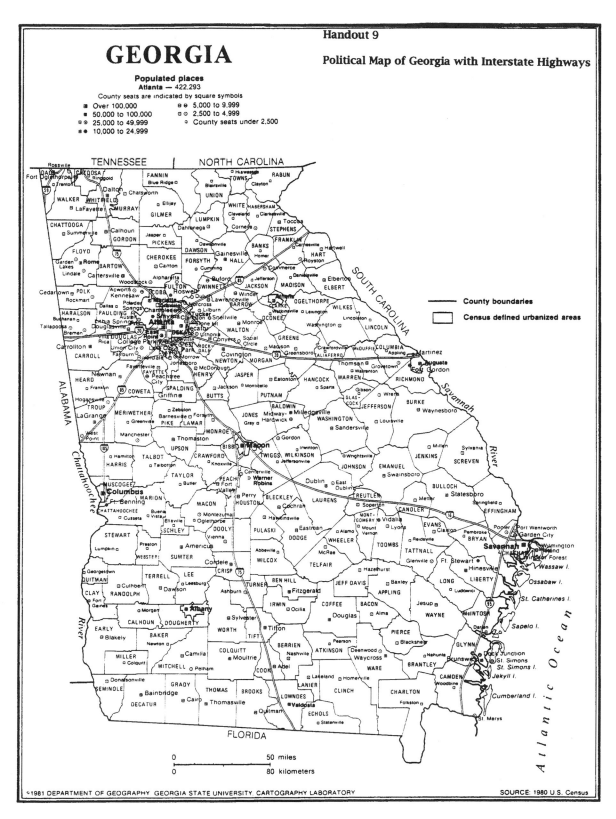

GEORGIA

Political Map of Georgia with Interstate Highways

Handout 9

Populated places
Atlanta — 422,293

County seats are indicated by square symbols

- Over 100,000
- 50,000 to 100,000
- 25,000 to 49,999
- 10,000 to 24,999
- 5,000 to 9,999
- 2,500 to 4,999
- County seats under 2,500

— County boundaries
☐ Census defined urbanized areas

0   50 miles
0   80 kilometers

©1981 DEPARTMENT OF GEOGRAPHY, GEORGIA STATE UNIVERSITY, CARTOGRAPHY LABORATORY

SOURCE: 1980 U.S. Census

UPD 8212/9-87

Political, Economic, Cultural, and Spatial Background Sheet (Handout 10)

Political Background for the Case Study

The consultants to the District Court have to consider a variety of political factors when partitioning the state's electoral space into congressional districts. For the case study, we will focus on three major factors. First the factor of political gerrymandering. The concept of gerrymandering is a political element that has had substantial influence throughout U.S. redistricting history. A gerrymandered district is an election district whose boundaries have been redrawn by the political party in power for its own political advantage. The word originated in 1812, during Elbridge Gerry's second term as governor of Massachusetts. Political gerrymandering of congressional districts persisted into the 1960s. In the Supreme Court case (*Reynolds v. Sims* 1964), the high court addressed the issue, prohibiting future political gerrymandering when drawing new congressional districts. The state legislature must adhere to this statute when creating new districts.

A second political factor the consultants to the District Court must consider is implementing and reacting to the Voting Rights Act of 1965 (or VRA). Since the passage of the VRA, the U.S. Department of Justice has had the obligation of enforcing the VRA and guaranteeing minority-group members the right to vote. Many states throughout the South reacted with an array of minority-vote dilution techniques, such as racial gerrymandering, to weaken minority political power in voting districts for popular representation in U.S. House of Representatives. The U.S. Supreme Court proceeded, through a series of court cases, to strengthen the Justice Department's power to fight vote dilution, and Congress in 1982 revised VRA. The Justice Department now had the authority to rearrange electoral space to safeguard newly enfranchised minority groups' ability to vote and control power. After the 1990 Census, the Justice Department took an aggressive role in the redistricting plans of the VRA-covered states in the South. The new majority-minority congressional districts in many states were disproportionate in shape that cut across well-recognized regional boundaries and ignored traditional communities of interest. The courts challenged these new congressional districts leading to a special redrawing in a few states. The Supreme Court in (*Miller v. Johnson* 1995) ruled that the 11th District in Georgia, drawn at the insistence of the Justice Department, was unconstitutional because race was the overriding factor in determining how the district's boundaries were drawn. Thus the state legislature must find a balance, include at least one majority-minority congressional district but without racial gerrymandering.

A third political factor the consultants to the District Court must consider is that each congressional district needs to be approximately uniform in population. This calculation in Georgia computes as the total population of 6,478,216 (1990 census) divided by eleven congressional districts, resulted in about 588,000 per district.

Economic Background for the Case Study

The first economic consideration the consultants to the District Court must consider is the concept of "communities of interest" that was approved by Supreme Court. The focus here is on Georgia's four traditional economic *corner* districts. Each of these regions has a common historic economic glue that provided a unity, which translated well into congressional districts. The court describes each corner district as:

1) the southeastern coastal district, comprising the coastal counties and the other counties most closely related to them.
2) an agrarian district in southwest Georgia, prominent for its peanut production.
3) the northwest corner, known for its carpet production and isolated from the northeast Georgia counties by mountains.
4) the northeastern corner, identified by its preeminence in poultry production.

These four districts are evident in the Congressional District Plans after the censuses of 1950, 1970, and 1980. The state legislature in our case study must take the "communities of interest" into consideration.

The second economic consideration the consultants to the District Court must consider is the emergence of new "community of interest" as a product of urban growth pushing from metropolitan Atlanta region towards the northeast along the Interstate 85 corridor. This fast growing group of suburban counties is sprawling into the metropolitan Athens area. The region's economic emergence translates well into a new congressional district.

Social Background for the Case Study

A social factor that the consultants to the District Court must consider is an extension of the VRA. They must consider the African-American population so that at least one majority-minority congressional district can be incorporated into the redistricting plan.

Spatial Background for the Case Study

The first spatial factor that the consultants to the District Court must consider is preserving entire counties within the districts. A possible exception could be made in one of the metropolitan Atlanta districts because of the difficulty of creating uniform population divisions.

The second spatial factor that the consultants to the District Court must consider is the concept of compactness. Each district should be spatially compact around population and communities of interest.

Political, Economic, Cultural and Spatial Background Response Sheet
(Handout 11)

1. Describe Gerrymandering.

2. How has the Voting Rights Act of 1965 affected the drawing of congressional districts in the United States?

3. What role has the United States Justice Department played in regard to the VRA?

4. Explain the conception of a majority-minority congressional district.

5. Describe the shape of Georgia's 11th congressional district after the 1990 census.

6. Describe the ruling in the Supreme Court case (Miller v. Johnson).

7. Explain your understanding of the Supreme Court's definition of "community of interest".

Congressional Maps through Time Response Sheet (Handout 12)

Congressional Map—1950 _____

Observation: _____

Number of Congressional Districts: _____

Patterns: _____

Shapes: _____

Speculation: Why does it look that way? _____

Congressional Map—1970

Observation: _____

Number of Congressional Districts: _____

Patterns: _____

Shapes: _____

Speculation: Why does it look that way? _____

Congressional Map—1980

Observation: _____

Number of Congressional Districts: _____

Patterns: _____

Shapes: _____

Speculation: Why does it look that way? _____

Congressional Map—1990

Observation: _____

Number of Congressional Districts: _____

Patterns: _____

Shapes: _____

Speculation: Why does it look that way? _____